TWENTIETH CENTURY INTERPRETATIONS
OF

MOBY-DICK

A Collection of Critical Essays

Edited by
MICHAEL T. GILMORE

Prentice-Hall, Inc.
A SPECTRUM BOOK   *Englewood Cliffs, N.J.*

Library of Congress Cataloging in Publication Data
Main entry under title:

Twentieth century interpretations of Moby-Dick; a collection of critical essays ①/①

  (A Spectrum Book)
see slip
  Bibliography: p. 121 - 123.
  1. Melville, Herman, 1819-1891. Moby-Dick.
I. Gilmore, Michael T. ②
PS2384.M62T9   813'.3   76-44426
ISBN 0-13-586057-1
ISBN 0-13-586032-6 pbk.

10 9 8 7 6 5 4 3 2 1

Prentice-Hall International, Inc., *London*
Prentice-Hall of Australia Pty. Limited, *Sydney*
Prentice-Hall of Canada, Ltd., *Toronto*
Prentice-Hall of India Private Limited, *New Delhi*
Prentice-Hall of Japan, Inc., *Tokyo*
Prentice-Hall of Southeast Asia Pte. Ltd., *Singapore*
Whitehall Books Limited, *Wellington, New Zealand*

Contents

PART TWO — *View Points*

Introduction

by Michael T. Gilmore

Moby-Dick is a book about man's attempt to understand and interpret his world, but it is a characteristically American book despite the universality of its theme. It addresses the problem of knowing in a context that is metaphysical rather than social or moral, and it invites comparison to such essentially philosophical works as Emerson's *Nature* (1836) and Poe's *Eureka* (1848), both of which evince a similar concern with the pursuit of ultimate "Truth" (a favorite word of Melville's and one which he was fond of capitalizing). In *Moby-Dick,* however, Melville does not share the confidence of his two compatriots in man's power to fathom the secrets of the universe. On the contrary, he challenges the notion that the meaning of existence can be discovered by man. The failure of Ahab's quest for the white whale expresses Melville's conviction that no correct interpretation of the cosmos can ever be found.

Melville's theme is introduced at the very beginning of the book, where his narrator Ishmael tries to account for his motives in going whaling. Declaring that "water and meditation are wedded for ever, "Ishmael suggests that the appeal of the sea lies in its association with "the ungraspable phantom of life" and thus with mankind's immemorial search for knowledge and meaning. Ishmael himself ships aboard the *Pequod* because he welcomes the opportunity to satisfy his curiosity about the whale. He is a rather bookish narrator who worked as a schoolmaster before becoming a sailor and who takes a scholar's delight in displaying his learning. He also has a scholar's interest in pursuing his education, and his curiosity about the whale extends to virtually the whole creation. "I want to see what whaling is," he tells Captain Peleg, "I want to see the world." He wants not simply to see, however, but to decipher what he sees: to uncover the hidden significance of things and events. He believes, for example, that

Father Mapple's actions upon ascending his pulpit "must symbolize something unseen," and he is no less determined than Ahab—or Emerson and Poe, for that matter—to arrive at some final understanding of man and the world. Before he even sets sail, he instinctively identifies his own quest for knowledge with Ahab's by relating "the ungraspable phantom of life" to Moby Dick. He first beholds the white whale looming mysteriously in his mind, "one grand hooded phantom, like a snow hill in the air."

Ahab of course is set upon vengeance, but he is also Melville's consummate "knower," and his hunt for the white whale may be regarded as an epistemological quest. When he first addresses the crew, he announces his intention to obtain knowledge by going beyond the limits of sensory data:

> All visible objects, man, are but as pasteboard masks. But in each event—in the living act, the undoubted deed—there, some unknown but still reasoning thing puts forth the mouldings of its features from behind the unreasoning mask. If man will strike, strike through the mask!

To Ahab, the white whale represents the mask or "wall" of natural phenomena which separates the inquiring mind from the thing-in-itself. Although he admits that there may be nothing beyond the wall of appearances—that nature may not be the symbol of spirit, as Emerson supposed, but only nature—he nevertheless vows to continue his quest whether the whale turns out to be "agent" or "principal." It is only by "thrusting through the wall," Ahab believes, that man can break free from his prison of ignorance.

Throughout *Moby-Dick*, Melville dwells on the connection between whaling and the pursuit of knowledge. In the chapter entitled "The Sphynx," for example, Ahab exhorts the severed head of a sperm whale to speak "and tell us the secret thing that is in thee. Of all divers, thou hast dived the deepest...thou hast seen enough to split the planets and make an infidel of Abraham...." Ishmael agrees that the whale is "physiognomically a Sphinx," and he implies that only the widsom of an Oedipus can solve the mystery of its brow, which is "pleated with riddles." Comparisons to philosophers and other eminent thinkers reinforce this impression of the whale as a repository of knowledge. Ishmael likens the head of the right whale to a Stoic and that of the sperm whale to "a Platonian, who might have taken up the study of Spinoza in his latter years." Discussing the mist emitted from the whale's spout, he conjectures that Plato, Pyrrho, and Dante all discharged a similar vapor while engaged in deep contemplation. He speaks of the whalemen themselves as "philosophers of the forecastle," and he says that the whaling industry has led the way in "ferreting out the remotest and least known parts of the earth." Is it any wonder, then, that Ishmael regards a whale ship as "my Yale College and my Harvard"?

Ishmael's wish to know the whale takes many forms, and his search impels him to swim through libraries as well as to sail through oceans. What he is forced to admit, however, is that his own efforts are no more availing than those of other men who have "thought, fancied, or sung of Leviathan." He first acknowledges as much in the chapter on "Cetology," and his confession of failure introduces a note that soon becomes a refrain. The chapter itself purports to be an exhaustive attempt at classifying all the known species of whales. It bristles with erudition from its opening list of the standard authorities to its division of the various species according to terms derived from printing. Yet Ishmael disclaims more than he claims for his system of classification. He says, in fact, that any human endeavor must necessarily fall short of completion, and he expresses his satisfaction at leaving his "cetological System standing thus unfinished." The dry, even pedantic tone of much of the chapter gives way to a prayer as Ishmael implores God to "keep me from ever finishing anything. This whole book is but a draught—nay, but the draught of a draught. Oh, Time, Strength, Cash, and Patience!"

One can best interpret Ishmael's words by placing them in the context of Melville's overall theme. It then becomes possible to substitute "epistemological" for "cetological" and to equate the system left unfinished with the search for knowledge. Ishmael himself invites this reading when he states elsewhere that the study of leviathan involves "the whole circle of the sciences" and embraces "the whole universe, not excluding its suburbs." The implication, to be developed inexorably as the tale proceeds, is that Truth in any comprehensive sense, Truth such as that sought by Ahab in his hunt for the white whale, is neither desirable nor attainable by man.

Certainly this is the inference encouraged by Ishmael as he continues his researches into the whale. It is not only books, he finds, but experience too that teaches the lesson of epistemological indeterminacy. In Chapter 68, "The Blanket," he takes up the vexed subject of the whale's skin, a topic as much debated by veteran whalemen as by learned naturalists on the shore. Reduced to venturing "only an opinion," he speculates that the whale's blubber is really its skin, and he adds that its fascination for the student of cetology stems from the linear markings which crisscross its surface. A first-hand inspection of these hieroglyphics merely confirms his suspicion that "the mystic-marked whale remains indecipherable." He meets with no better success when he turns to the spout and tries to determine the composition of its vapory jet. "You might almost stand in it," he writes, "and yet be undecided as to what it is precisely." No such experiment is likely to be undertaken, however, because of the physical danger of coming into contact with the acrid mist. "The wisest thing the investigator can do then, it seems to me, is to let this deadly spout alone."

Ishmael's efforts to understand the rest of the whale invariably reach the same conclusion. The chapters dealing with other parts of the anatomy like the head and the tail typically begin by setting forth a mass of evidence and end by admitting the impossibility of full comprehension. After carefully examining the whale's forehead, Ishmael despairs of ever unriddling "the awful Chaldee" of its brow. His scrutiny of the tail proves just as unfruitful: "the more I consider this mighty tail, the more do I deplore my inability to express it." Nor does he confine his explorations to the whale's exterior. Several years before the voyage of the *Pequod,* he visited a bower in the Arsacides where the skeleton of a sperm whale had been preserved as a temple, and he was able to make a thorough study of its innermost structure. But poring over the whale's skeleton and measuring its length added little to his understanding of the living creature: "No. Only in the heart of quickest perils; only within the eddyings of his angry flukes; only on the profound unbounded sea, can the fully invested whale be truly and livingly found out."

The assurance of this last passage is undercut by the fact that even on the unbounded sea the whale eludes comprehension. Ishmael's experiences as a whaleman strengthen rather than diminish his skepticism, and make him contemptuous of the rival epistemologies of Locke and Kant, the two philosophers most familiar to Melville's contemporaries. A right whale's head has been hoisted on the port side of the *Pequod* to balance the weight of a sperm whale's head on the starboard. Noting the ship's difficulty in staying afloat, Ishmael observes that the student of practical cetology who figuratively hoists in the heads of Locke and Kant will find himself in as sorry a plight. "Oh, ye foolish! throw all these thunderheads overboard, and then you will float light and right." In Emerson's terms, the whale can neither be known by Lockian Understanding nor apprehended through Kantian Reason. Experientially, the whale cannot be known at all: "I know him not, and never will."

Art may succeed where experience fails in conveying an accurate view of the whale. Ishmael explores this possibility by describing the pictures of artists who have tried to capture the whale on canvas. He runs through a lengthy list of illustrations only to dismiss them all as "pictorial delusions," and he concludes his survey by reiterating his proscription against the pursuit of epistemological completeness:

> So there is no earthly way of finding out precisely what the whale really looks like. And the only mode in which you can derive even a tolerable idea of his living contour is by going a whaling yourself; but by so doing, you run no small risk of being eternally stove and sunk by him. Wherefore, it seems to me you had best not be too fastidious in your curiosity touching this Leviathan.

Since the whale is intrinsically unknowable, it "must remain unpainted to the last."

Language, the medium of literature, is no more reliable than brushwork in enabling the would-be knower to make sense of his world. In Chapter 99, "The Doubloon," Ishmael says that "some certain significance lurks in all things," and he recounts the efforts of Ahab, Starbuck, and others to elucidate the meaning of the gold coin nailed to the mainmast. Each observer interprets the coin subjectively, limited as he is by his own perceptions, and each uses language accordingly. Pip, who is said to have been studying his grammar, dramatizes the difficulty of objective perception by conjugating the verb to look: "I look, you look, he looks; we look, ye look, they look." Melville rejects the Emersonian creed that words are signs of natural objects because he recognizes that dissimilar individuals, not to mention dissimilar peoples, perceive the world differently and use different words in speaking of the identical objects. To underscore this point, he begins *Moby-Dick* with a section on etymology in which he reprints the word for whale in Hebrew, Greek, Latin, and so on. A

brief sketch of the "late consumptive usher" who supposedly supplied the etymology spells out the moral of human fallibility:

> The pale Usher—threadbare in coat, heart, body, and brain; I see
> him now. He was ever dusting his old lexicons and grammars, with
> a queer hankerchief, mockingly embellished with all the gay
> flags of all the known nations of the world. He loved to dust his
> old grammars; it somehow mildly reminded him of his mortality.

In brief: Ishmael's warning in "Cetology" that man is inherent-
ly limited, and that his desire for full comprehension can never
be gratified, is Melville's answer to the epistemological question
raised by Ahab's symbolic hunt. The outcome of *Moby-Dick,* in
which the white whale escapes, demonstrates the futility of Ahab's
quest and reaffirms the inscrutability of existence. It makes a
mockery of the Captain's boast that "Truth hath no confines."
This "ungodly, god-like man" who is "gifted with the high perception," who aspires to be an Oedipus, and who vows to solve
the riddle of the Parsee's disappearance, suffers the same fate that
befell the original Oedipus as punishment for his hubris. "I grow
blind," he exclaims just moments before his death, "hands! stretch
out before me that I may yet grope my way. Is't night?" A blind
man hurling himself against the impregnable wall of a monstrous
sperm whale—this is Melville's metaphor for the futile effort to
interpret the world. The "ungraspable phantom of life" is forever
ungraspable; "and this is the key to it all."

One figure does escape from the wreck of the *Pequod* to tell the
story of Ahab's disastrous encounter with Moby Dick. Melville's
narrator Ishmael, the orphan and wanderer who asked God to
prevent him from completing anything, is saved by a riddle. As
the last chip of the ship is drawn toward the fatal vortex, the black
bubble bursts and releases the coffin life-buoy that keeps him
afloat on the dirgelike sea. The coffin is inscribed with a copy
of the tattooing that adorns Queequeg's body and that contains
"a complete theory of the heavens and the earth." But these
hieroglyphical markings, like those on the whale, are indecipherable, "so that Queequeg in his own proper person was a
riddle to unfold; a wondrous work in one volume" whose mysteries are destined to "be unsolved to the last."

A wanderer is one who never completes his journey, and an
orphan has no final home nor place to rest. By ending *Moby-
Dick* with the word "orphan," Melville reemphasizes the im-

possibility of finding a conclusive solution to the riddle of the universe. Ishmael himself says that all men are figurative orphans who seek in vain for the secret of their paternity and who voyage eternally in pursuit of "the final harbor, whence we unmoor no more." Like Hawthorne, for whom Melville professed such extravagant admiration in his famous review of *Mosses from an Old Manse*, Ishmael adopts the attitude of "a seeker, not a finder yet." *Moby-Dick* itself, he claims, is an unfinished book—"but the draught of a draught"—because it depicts a quest whose object, the whale, defies complete understanding and remains an enigma to man.

When *Moby-Dick* was published in 1851, Evert Duyckinck, Melville's friend and the editor of the New York *Literary World*, complained that "it becomes quite impossible to submit such books to a distinct classification as fact, fiction, or essay." Duyckinck was wrong to pronounce *Moby-Dick* a failure, but he was right to suggest that it baffles interpretation. Like the white whale itself, it is neither "a monstrous fable" nor "a hideous and intolerable allegory," and it resists any effort to reduce it to a single meaning. In this respect it resembles the grimy and defaced oil painting discovered by Ishmael in the Spouter Inn of New Bedford. Unable at first to make out the painting's subject, Ishmael speculates that the artist "had endeavored to delineate chaos bewitched." After careful study, however, and not without feeling that his initial impression is correct, he offers a "theory" that the picture depicts a mortal combat between whale and whaler. *Moby-Dick* is about a comparable struggle, and any reading that attempts to fathom its mysteries can be no more than a partial and incomplete theory. "A sort of indefinite, half-attained, unimaginable sublimity" is characteristic of the book as well as the painting, and rules out epistemological certainty on the part of the reader. There is reason to believe that Melville wished *Moby-Dick* to produce this effect. His next book, appropriately enough, was entitled *Pierre; or, The Ambiguities*, and his last, *Billy Budd*, was left unfinished at his death.

Harry Levin once observed that "the investigation of *Moby-Dick* might almost be said to have taken the place of whaling among the industries of New England." The industry is still thriving, and as the selections in this volume indicate, it is hardly confined to New England or even the United States. I hope that the samples of criticism included here will give some idea of the variety and scope of Melville scholarship over the past fifty years. Considerations of space unfortunately dictated the omission of several outstanding essays, two of which deserve particular mention: D. H. Lawrence's chapter on *Moby-Dick* in *Studies in Classic American Literature* (1923), and Henry A. Murray's "In Nomine Diaboli," *New England Quarterly,* 24 (December 1951), 435-52. The Lawrence book is available in a paperback edition; Murray's essay has been reprinted in numerous anthologies, including Richard Chase, ed., *Melville: A Collection of Critical Essays* (Englewood Cliffs, N.J.: Prentice-Hall, 1962).

The Romantic Use of Symbols

by W. H. Auden

To understand the romantic conception of the relation between objective and subjective experience, *Moby-Dick* is perhaps the best work to study, partly because in certain aspects it includes preromantic attitudes and treatments which show off the former more clearly than a purely romantic work like *The Ancient Mariner* or *Gordon Pym*.

If we omit the White Whale itself, the whole book is an elaborate synecdoche, i.e., it takes a particular way of life, that of whale-fishing, which men actually lead to earn their livelihood and of which Melville had first-hand experience and makes it a case of any man's life in general. This literary device is an old one and can be found at all periods; indeed almost all literature does this.

E.g.

1. Whalemen kill for their living. So in one way or another must we all.

2. The proprietors of the *Pequod* are Quakers, i.e., they profess the purest doctrine of non-violence, yet see no incongruity in this; though perhaps Peleg recognises the paradox indirectly when he says: "Pious Harpooners never make good voyages. It takes the shark out of them." So always in every life, except that of the saint or the villain, there is a vast difference between what a man professes and how he acts.

3. The crew are involved in each other's actions and characters. So every world is a world of social relations.

4. In their attitude towards their job of killing whales, they reveal their different characters. Thus Starbuck is a professional

who takes no risks unless he has to and will have no man in his
boat who is not afraid of the whale. Stubb is a reckless gambler who
enjoys risks. Flask follows the fish just for the fun of it.

Insofar as the book is this, any other form of activity or society
which Melville happened to know well would have served his
purpose.

Then *Moby-Dick* is full of parable and typology, i.e., as X is in
one field of experience, so is Y in another.

E.g.

All men live enveloped in whale-lines. All are born with halters
round their necks; but it is only when caught in the soft, sudden
turn of death that mortals realise the silent subtle ever-present
perils of life.   (Chapter LX)

or

O men, admire—model thyself after the whale. Do thou too remain warm among ice. Do thou, too, live in this world without being
of it. Be cool at the Equator, keep thy blood flow at the Pole and
retain in all seasons a temperature of thine own.

(Chapter LXVIII)

or again the characters and names of the nine ships (the number
is symbol not allegory) which the *Pequod* encounters are, in their
relation to Moby Dick, types of the relation of human individuals
and societies in the tragic mystery of existence. I.e.,

The *Goney*	The aged who may have experienced the mystery but cannot tell others. (The captain's trumpet falls into the sea.)
The *Town-Ho*	Those who have knowledge of the mystery but keep it secret. (No one tells Ahab the story of Radney and Steelkilt.)
The *Jeroboam*	Those who make a superstitious idolatry of the mystery or whom the mystery has driven crazy.
The *Jungfrau* and the *Rosebud*	Those who out of sloth and avarice respectively will never become aware of the mystery.

The *Enderby*	Those who are aware of the mystery but face it with rational common sense and stoicism. ("What you take for the White Whale's malice is only his awkwardness.")
The *Bachelor*	The frivolous and fortunate who deny the existence of the mystery. ("Have heard of Moby Dick but don't believe in him at all.")
The *Rachel*	Those who have without their understanding or choice become involved in the mystery as the innocents massacred by Herod were involved in the birth of Christ.
The *Delight*	Those whose encounter with the mystery has turned their joy into sorrow.

This analogical method was practised by the Church Fathers in their interpretations of Scripture, and analogies from nature have been common ever since, for example in the Mediaeval Bestiaries or Jonathan Edwards' *Images or Shadows of Divine Things*. It is a conscious process, calling for Judgment and Fancy rather than Imagination, and the one-to-one correspondence asserted is grasped by the reader's reason.

Lastly, in his treatment of the White Whale, Melville uses symbols in the real sense.

A symbol is felt to be such before any possible meaning is consciously recognised; i.e., an object or event which is felt to be more important than the reason can immediately explain is symbolic. Secondly, a symbolic correspondence is never one to one but always multiple, and different persons perceive different meanings. Thus to Ahab "All visible objects, man, are but pasteboard masks. To me the white whale is that wall shoved near to me. Sometimes I think there's naught beyond. I see in him outrageous strength with an insatiable malice sinewing it. That inscrutable thing is chiefly what I hate."

To Gabriel, the mad demagogue who terrorises the *Jeroboam*, its qualities are similar, but his attitude is one of positive idolisation. He worships it as an incarnation of the Shaker God. To Steelkilt of the *Town-Ho* it is the justice and mercy of God, saving him from   coming a murderer and slaying the unjust Radney. To Melville-Ishmael it is neither evil nor good but simply numinous, a declaration of the power and majesty of God which transcends any human standards of ethics. To Starbuck it signifies death or his fatal relation to his captain, the duty which tells him he cannot depart his office to obey, intending open war, yet to have a touch of pity.

Moby-Dick: The American National Epic

by Richard Slotkin

In *Moby-Dick* the American epic takes the form of a colossal hunt. All the elements of the hunter myth are developed to their archetypal extremes. The mythic characterization of the wilderness as a symbol of primal states of nature and of human consciousness had been distilled by Cooper (in the last Leather-stocking tale) and Thoreau into the image of the lake (Glimmer-glass) or pond (Walden)—bodies of water which reflect the features of heroes and contain mysteries in their depths; sources of the forest's life and repositories of death's victims. In Melville's novel Glimmerglass/Walden becomes ocean itself; and Cooper's oceanic prairie and forest become metaphors by which Melville defines the vastness of his ocean and the relatedness of the *Pequod's* hunt to the mythologized adventures of Boone and Leatherstocking. The object of his quest is likewise magnified. No deer or loon embodies in microcosm the spirit of a natural divinity, but Levia-than himself, a beast like an island or a continent in the middle ocean, a creature sometimes worshiped as the godhead itself. These expansions, which represent the ultimate development of the terms of the hunting myth, in fact restore original elements of the dream of the West that impelled the first discoveries—the dream of the mystic islands in the ocean-sea that hold both the possibility of eternal bliss and godlike power and the potential for utter death and damnation. In the end is the beginning.

This return to basic archetypal terms, however, does not imply a denial of the changes and developments of the hunter myth in America during the intervening years. Rather, the novel gathers

"Moby-Dick: The American National Epic" by Richard Slotkin. From *Regeneration Through Violence: The Mythology of the American Frontier, 1600-1860,* by Richard Slotkin (Middletown, Conn.: Wesleyan University Press, 1973), pp. 539-50. Copyright © 1973 by Richard Slotkin. Reprinted by permission of the publisher.

together the variant strands and images of the myth and relates them to one another, to the central myth that underlies them, and to the history that has been shaped by the myth over the previous two centuries of American history. The myth of the hunter, as we have seen it develop in America, has centered on the theme of initiation into a new life, a new world, a new stage of manhood. This initiation has been variously imagined as a Puritan religious conversion, or as a cannibal Eucharist unifying the spirit of the white man with that of the Indian wilderness, or as a sacred marriage sexually linking the hero and the woods-goddess, or as a novice's or a boy's initiation into the mysteries and skills of the natural powers. Within each of these variants of the initiation theme, characteristic polarities and conflicts exist, centering on the difference between the Christian and the primitive-mythopoeic approaches to envisioning the wilderness and living in it. Each of these variants of the myth figures in Melville's novel, as does the central conflict of vision, and each is framed by the story of Ishmael's (the narrator-persona's) initiation.

Ishmael is a novice at whaling, and the voyage of the *Pequod* is his initiation into its lore and its arts. The reader is also entered upon a careful initiation into whaling, since Ishmael, like an old hand, carefully and patiently explains both the function and the mythology connected with the activities, gear, and tackle of the whaling trade. However, we are warned at the outset that this double initiation is not simply into the activity of the whaleman's life. "Meditation and water are wedded for ever," says Ishmael, in the chapter called "Loomings,"[1] and the whaling voyage opens up for us not only the outward but the inward ocean as well. Before Moby Dick appears on the physical horizon—indeed, before Ishmael has even seen the seacoast or the whaler or heard the name of Moby Dick—the goal of the quest looms mysteriously in his mind:

> Chief among these motives was the overwhelming idea of the great whale himself. Such a portentous and mysterious monster roused all my curiosity.... The great flood-gates of the wonder-world swung open, and in the wild conceits that swayed me to my purpose, two and two there floated into my inmost soul, endless processions of

[1]Herman Melville, *Moby-Dick*, p. 2. (Citations to *Moby-Dick* are from the Modern Library Edition—editor's note.)

the whale, and, mid most of them all, one grand hooded phantom, like a snow hill in the air.[2]

Ishmael's mind moves toward this prophetic vision, Melville suggests, by a mental process as instinctual and archetypal as that which draws men and streams down to the ocean that is their source and ending. Intellection is powerless to discover any adequate substitute for the sea-hunger. In deciding on a whaling voyage, intellectual "curiosity" is Ishmael's first motive, as it was Filson's Boone's. But, as with Flint's Boone, even before he has begun to satisfy that curiosity, the mythic form of his object begins to take shape in his mind. His image of the "processions of the whale" couches that vision in almost Indian terms: the group of creatures, appearing in a revery, are identified by their species name (not as individual, plural "whales"), and that species is headed by its archetypal grandfather in the shape of a solitary, unpaired, and unwedded whale, the phantom mountain-shape he later knows as Moby Dick.

Melville draws heavily on the island mythology that characterized both the prediscovery European myths of the West and the later images of island colonies in the oceanic forest. This imagery is also clarified and heightened by Melville to bring out its last significations. All great continents are but islands in the sea— enclosures of light, order, and peace in a dark, fundamental, all-creating, all-dissolving ocean. So the reasoning mind of man is an isolated enclosure amid the chaos of his emotions. Within that mind are ideas that are themselves like islands, offering intellectual refuge from the daily tragedy of existence—the dream-remembered, womblike haven of an innocent childhood, ruled and ordered by a maternal figure; or the dream-longed-for "Tahiti" with which the exiled soul stays its hunger for refuge, peace, and completion. To leave the maternal home for the life of a mature man, or to allow the soul to venture out of the secure solitude of the ego's mental Tahiti in search of human love, is to immerse oneself in the destructive element, to expose oneself to passion, degradation, and dissolution: "For as this appalling ocean surrounds the verdant land, so in the soul of man there lies one insular Tahiti, full of peace and joy, but encompassed by all

[2]Ibid., p. 6.

the horrors of the half known life. God keep thee! Push not off
from that isle, thou canst never return!"[3]

Each of the main characters in the novel is an islander of sorts—
which is to say, in contradiction to Donne, that each man *is* an
island. Ahab and Starbuck are Nantucketers, Stubb a Cape-
Codder (nearly an island), Flask a Vineyarder, Ishmael from
Manhattan, Queequeg a Polynesian, Tashtego a Vineyarder.
"They were nearly all Islanders in the Pequod, *Isolatoes* too...not
acknowledging the common continent of men, but each...living
on a separate continent of his own."[4] Even the African Daggoo is
an islander, for the continents themselves are but islands in the
universal ocean. The whale himself, we are told, is often mistaken
for an island.

What relationship can islanded man have with the ocean that
sustains or, at a whim, destroys him? Crèvecoeur, in his study of
Nantucket, suggests that man can farm the physical ocean as he
cultivates the land, thus bringing it under the rule of his skill.
Crèvecoeur offers the island of Nantucket as proof of what reason-
able cultivation can produce. Melville, however, sees Nantucket
as a product of man's mythically motivated confrontation with
the irrational, oceanic forces of nature. Melville's brief history
of Nantucket begins with an Indian legend about its discovery;
and his Nantucketer is pictured as a man at home only on the sea,
an absolute stranger to land, a man whose life and labor embody
the island nature of all human life, both mental and metaphysical:
"so at nightfall, the Nantucketer, out of sight of land, furls his
sails, and lays him to his rest, while under his very pillow rush
herds of walruses and whales."[5]

Not all men can live on such accepting terms with their island
nature. The Negro cabin boy, Pip, deserted in the ocean, discovers his island nature with a vengeance. The vast oceanic universe enters his mind and devours it, drowning reason in
an all-encompassing, ineluctable experience of cosmic reality:

> The sea had jeeringly kept his finite body up, but drowned the in-
> finite of his soul. Not drowned entirely, though. Rather carried
> down alive to wondrous depths, where strange shapes of the un-

[3]Ibid., p. 276.

[4]Ibid., p. 119

[5]Ibid., p. 63.

warped primal world glided to and fro before his passive eyes; and the miser-merman, Wisdom, revealed his hoarded heaps; and among the joyous, heartless, ever-juvenile eternities, Pip saw the multitudinous, God-omnipresent, coral insects, that out of the firmament of waters heaved the colossal orbs. He saw God's foot upon the treadle of the loom, and spoke it; and therefore his shipmates called him mad. So man's insanity is heaven's sense; and wandering from all mortal reason, man comes at last to that celestial thought, which, to reason, is absurd and frantic; and weal or woe, feels then uncompromised, indifferent as his God.[6]

Pip, in other words, has been mentally drowned in the primal, archetypal realm (Moira). In that encounter he has perceived and been reconciled to the cosmogonic powers and processes of the natural universe. But the god he beholds is neither man nor demon. Rather, that god is figured in the image of the teeming, nonhuman, unindividuated multitudes of the coral insects, whose pyramided skeletons—piled by blind process, not purpose—are the substance of the islands that are the orbs or worlds of the ocean-universe.

Ahab, a man proud of his Promethean or Faustian reason, cannot be passive in acceptance of reality, as Pip is. Always he seeks to impose his reason—by imposing reasons—on the blank, unintelligible face of the natural universe or the featureless front of the faceless whale.[7] Only the whale is adjusted to his island nature and able to maintain some integrity of soul in the chaotic sea. Moby Dick is apparently immortal in his solitude. Lesser whales, traveling in herds, build a kind of social order that takes its pattern from the island-sea relationship. In "The Grand Armada" the whalemen enter the "charmed circle" at the center of the whale herd: while stricken and angered leviathans rage at the circumference, the cows and calves and the amorous, breeding young swim in an "enchanted," enclosed, and protected island-pond. Even the bloody whalemen are moved to sympathy. Queequeg is especially moved to pat the foreheads of the young whales and Starbuck to scratch their backs with his lance. It is a Nantucket vision of the earthy paradise.

The stages of Ishmael's initiation offer Melville an opportunity to develop his and his reader's symbolic vocabulary, making the

[6]Ibid., p. 413.
[7]Ibid., pp. 335-36, 344.

novel as independent of exterior frames of reference as possible, making it an island of a book—self-sufficient, self-explaining, and self-justifying like all myth. Through Ishmael's observations, his actions, and his metaphorical descriptions of whaling activities and equipment, an elaborate structure of interlocking mythological and metaphorical systems or thematic streams is established; and these are unified in the course of the observer's dual initiation into whaling and wisdom.

The American popular mythology forms one such stream of metaphor, linking the hunting of the whale to the mythology of explorers, hunters, and Indian fighters. Ishmael's Boone-like approach to the threshold of adventure has already been cited. His subsequent actions also smack of the frontier myth. Of all places to begin his quest, Ishmael chooses Nantucket because it was the primitive source of American whaling, the island from which "those aboriginal whalemen, the Red-Men, first sall[ied] out in canoes to give chase to Leviathan."[8] The ship Ishmael chooses to voyage in is the *Pequod,* named for the tribe massacred by the Puritans in 1638 and now the island and vessel of successors of both Puritan and pagan, united in a mutual quest. The captain of the ship, Ahab, is both Quaker and hunter, like Boone himself and like Bird's Nathan Slaughter. The object of his hunt, Moby Dick, has a forehead like "the prairie" and a hump like a buffalo. The whale's resemblance to the prairie marks him as the true avatar of the essential spirit of his element, for the sea is also called "prairie," "meadow," and "desert." As his hunter resembles Boone, so is Moby Dick, as chief of the order of solitary bull whales, compared with "moss-bearded Daniel Boone." The whalemen snatch their harpoons from the crotch as quickly "as a backwoodsman swings his rifle from the wall." The white whale is compared to the "White Steed" in the popular fiction of western magazines, and "your true whale hunter is as much a savage as an Iroquois."[9]

The use of this frontier metaphor, however, is not restricted to imagery and motif merely. The central concern of the epic is to illuminate the motives and consequences—the very nature—of the archetypal myths that undergulf these American legends.

---

[8]Ibid., p. 7.

[9]See ibid., pp. 189, 289, 343, 392. For a full account of Melville's uses of frontier sources and images, see Edwin Fussell, *Frontier: American Literature and the American West* (Princeton, N.J.: Princeton University Press, 1966), pp. 256-80.

The frontier motif is therefore made to function as a subordinate aspect of the archetypal myths of the Eucharist and the sacred marriage and of Ishmael's gradual discovery of their presence and power in the world of the *Pequod*. The marriage metaphor is the more crucial of the two, since the cannibal Eucharist is a ritual sublimation of the mutual sexual absorption of hero and goddess. Both myths are essentially myths of fertility—of the procreation, preservation, perpetuation, and resurrection of human and animal life. Ishmael begins his quest because there is a winter, a "November" in his soul; he seeks the spring and the resurrection of life through his quest. In his vision the whales appear to him in wedded pairs, and in the first stages of his initiation he finds himself embracing the cannibal king Queequeg, wielder of a mighty harpoon, as bride embraces husband. The object of their quest is the sperm whale, whose very name suggests a titanic, phallic power of procreation. Queequeg's rescue of a fallen harpooner from the sperm well of a severed whale's head is described as an act of rebirth, a resurrection of the fallen man from the womblike well of the whale's "tun." One of the most erotic scenes in nineteenth-century American literature is that in which Ishmael and his fellows bathe their hands in sperm oil to squeeze out impurities and experience an exquisite, sensual melting-together of characters and sympathies.

The nature and significance of cannibalism is slowly unveiled in a similar manner. The association of cannibalism and whaling seems, in the first marriage of Queequeg and Ishmael, simply to refer to the primitive basis of the whale- or man-hunting instinct. The discovery of the *Pequod* expands the motif. Her rig and appearance partake of the mysteries of Japan and Gothic Europe. Her decorations of whalebone, however, mark her as worthy of her Indian name. "She was a thing of trophies. A cannibal of a craft, tricking herself forth in the chased bones of her enemies."[10] The Pequot Indians, suppressed by the fathers of these Nantucketers, thus have their final triumph. As the Pequots decked themselves in scalps, so their white heirs (like Benjamin Church) deck their ship in the name of their slaughtered foe and make their ship a cannibal as well. The motif further unfolds its meaning in "Stubb's Supper," in which the mate eats a steak from the whale he has killed, imbibing its power with its flesh in the Indian manner. In so doing he associates himself with the sea-

[10]*Moby-Dick*, p. 69.

hounds, the obscene self- and fellow-devouring sharks who harry the stricken whales and, in their hunger-lust, pervertedly devour their own entrails when wounded.

The marriage and cannibal metaphors, and the mythic strains they represent, provide the context in which the problem of the great hunter-captain Ahab slowly reveals itself. The act of eating and drinking the body and blood in the Eucharist is meant as an act of love, uniting a worshiper with a beloved deity; the sacred marriage that consummates the hunt is likewise meant as a loving consummation. Hunters like Actaeon, Orion, and the unfortunate brave in the Sioux legend of the White Buffalo Woman— those who approach the hunt with lust or hatred in their hearts — are destroyed, and the rites of love are thwarted or consummated in annihilation. Ahab's hatred of the thing he hunts violates the ethic of the hunter myth, in which the hunter and the beast are lovingly to share and interchange identities. As in *Nick of the Woods*, the conflict is between the points of view represented by the captivity mythology of the Puritans and the hunting mythology of the Indians and frontiersmen. In the former man is either passive victim or agent of vengeance, either Quaker or slaughterer. In the latter he is the lover of the thing he hunts.

Ahab and his intended prey are doubles. Both have ribbed brows, wry mouths, and withered or stricken limbs. Both share an apparent spirit of conscious malice that goes beyond the natural, instinctual violence of whalemen like Starbuck and Stubb and of normal whales. The root of malice is in both cases the same: Ahab has been wounded and maimed by the whale, and the whale by whalemen. Both are driven into isolation, away from the normal life of marriage and begetting: Moby Dick is a solitary whale, Ahab leaves wife and babes to pursue his vengeance. Both share a common mystery or ambivalence in their nature. Ahab is both victim and hero, Quaker and killer, Christian and blood-lusting pagan. Moby Dick is similarly enigmatic and mysterious, both animal and spirit, unconscious and conscious in malice, instinctual and intelligent, the exile from the whale-herd's "charmed circle" and the rescuer of hunted females, the victim of men and the destroyer of men. Ahab identifies Moby Dick as being either the "principle" or the "agent" of the inscrutable but malicious power that rules the universe. Similarly, in his conversation with Starbuck in "The Symphony," he identifies his own case in these terms, torn between the idea that he is the "principle" in the quest and the willful controller of its action and the contrary idea that he is the "agent" of some outside force: "Is Ahab, Ahab? Is it I, God, or who, that lifts this arm?"[11] One thing only divides them: it is possible that the whale is, as Starbuck says (and as Pip's vision implies), a mere beast.

Ahab's pursuit of the whale with murderous intent is thus a compounded violation of nature. If there is no reasoning intelligence behind the events of life, then Ahab's quest is the projection of a madman's vision on the neutral face of reality, a denial of that "atheism" of the natural universe represented by "the Whiteness of the Whale."[12] If the associations that link Ahab and the whale are emblems of their common creaturehood (whether of an integral deity or of the soulless deities of Pip's vision), then the hunt is a symbolic fratricide; and since kinship suggests a fundamental sharing of identity, the hunt is also an act of self-destruction, so that the whale blood Ahab hopes to drink will perversely be his own. The choice that opens before him involves a choice of approaches to the beast. Will he come as a metaphysician-madman—a self-willed, self-devouring, perverted hunter-shark, bent on obscenity and evil—or as a worshiper and lover?

Melville binds the characters of Ahab and the whale by the cords of mystery, by involving us in the task of unraveling a riddle of appearance and reality. The chapters on the whale present no definitive view of him; rather, they view him from every conceivable viewpoint, portray him in every conceivable shape, denying none and accepting none. By the time the whale is sighted, his character has been established as protean and many-leveled. Ishmael has shown him to us as agent of God, as avatar of God, as God himself. He has also shown him as he appears to Ahab and to the objective scientist or the fact-minded Starbuck. Is the whale God, or avatar of the gods of the wilderness-sea, or simple beast, or projection of Ahab's own mind, avatar of the hunter's own soul? And if he is any of these, what ought Ahab's response to the whale be? If a God or avatar of a god, should Ahab not worship him? If an animal, should he not ignore him? If a projection of his own mind, should he not seek to comprehend and be reconciled to him?

The choice that confronts Ahab as the chase nears its end is couched in the terms of the marriage metaphor that has informed

[11] Ibid., pp. 534-35.
[12] Ibid., pp. 194-95.

the structure of the epic. Under the aspect of this myth, Moby
Dick is either an avatar of the nature goddess, embodying a
principle of fertility, or else the objective correlative of the anima,
the necessary feminine component of Ahab's own mind—or both
at once. Ishmael, unfolding some more of his whale lore to the
reader, gives us the features of Ahab and his dilemma reflected
in the mirror of the whale world. The sperm whale is a creature
of schools and societies, a *pater familias* and affectionate mate
during his youth. But in his crabbed age, when wounds and years
have weakened his procreative powers (thus enforcing the chastity
prized by Thoreau and Leatherstocking) and declining vigor and
health torment him, he becomes a solitary hermit. Melville expresses this in terms of the Boone myth and the myth of the
hunter's sacred marriage: "Almost universally, a lone whale—
as a solitary Leviathan is called—proves an ancient one. Like
venerable moss-bearded Daniel Boone, he will have no one near
him but Nature herself; and her he takes to wife in the wilderness
of waters, and the best of wives she is, though she keeps so many
moody secrets."[13]

The sperm whale at each stage thus has his appropriate mate,
the younger in whale society, the older in a more mystical and
mythological union with the goddess of nature herself, the earned
result of a life spent in perfect accordance with the gifts of nature.
Ahab, by this standard, is guilty of violating natural law. An aged,
crabbed man, he has taken a young woman to wife, solacing himself for his time-bound decline in vigor as King David did, by
taking young virgins to bed. Even so, she is a more appropriate
wife for him than the whale or god or goddess he seeks; and his
leaving her widowed when he still might be a true husband is a
crime equivalent to a paternal whale's deserting his "harem."
Enforced chastity (through age or isolation) or perversely motivated chastity converts Thoreau's "saving virtue" into corruption
and destruction of the loving motives that should underlie the
hunter's acts. Ahab seeks only to be wedded to Moby Dick by the
binding cord of the harpoon line, but hate drives him, and he is
fleeing from his true "haven" behind. He wants no communion
with unknowable divine mystery, no wife and moody secrets. His
purpose is to dispel mystery with cruel and metallic analysis, to
"strike through the mask" of the whale and murder its symbolic
essence. He has been wounded by the whale as by time, and his

[13]Ibid., p. 392.

response to both wounds, both diminutions of his vigor, is violence, hatred, and repudiation rather than love. When, on the eve of the sighting of Moby Dick, Starbuck offers Ahab the choice between the image of his proper love, his wife, and the image of his hatred, Ahab hesitates. Then, looking into the mirroring sea ("meditation and water are wedded forever") to behold his own features, he declares for vengeance and destruction rather than love. All around him, sky and sea marry in a unity which (as Melville describes it) is a coitus of cosmic sexual principles.

The whale can be the source of either salvation or damnation to Ahab. As an avatar of the goddess of nature and the double of Ahab, Moby Dick mediates between the man and the divine. Ahab rejects the hope of a mediator and puts his faith in the direct confrontation of man and god in mortal strife, with salvation and immortality as the stake.

The identity of the whale, at which Ishmael has been hinting, is suddenly revealed. The whale appears to Ahab and the crew as the very vision and embodiment of the god and goddess of wilderness nature and of the dreams of the subconscious mind, which the Puritans so feared to release, express, or give opportunity to escape. The whale is at once masculine and feminine, a phallus and an odalisque, enticing and overwhelmingly erotic, recalling the fertility myths of the Greeks in which beast-gods mate with human virgins:

> A gentle joyousness—a mighty mildness of repose in swiftness, invested the gliding whale. Not the white bull Jupiter swimming away with ravished Europa clinging to his graceful horns; his lovely, leering eyes sideways intent upon the maid; with smooth bewitching fleetness, rippling straight for the nuptial bower in Crete; not Jove, not that great majesty Supreme! did surpass the glorified White Whale as he so divinely swam.[14]

Three times Ahab, seduced by this vision, assails the whale to kill it. On the third try the whale ceases to restrain its power and reveals its full majesty to destroy Ahab, ship, men, and all in universal catastrophe. On each day of the chase the alternative choice is renewed to Ahab—to cease his hatred of the whale, to lovingly accept and worship its power and the power it represents, and to give over the chase and return to his proper wife. Each day he declines that choice, seeing in the whale only the em-

[14]Ibid., p. 538.

bodiment of the darker impulses of man and of nature—of Ahab and Ahab's God—that he wishes to obliterate. His response to the spirit of nature is that of the Puritan: he is either its captive and victim or the agent of a transcendent power that destroys it. He worships, not the whale or the god, but the wound they gave him; and he does not seek healing so much as vengeance. As a Puritan he perverts the hunter myth, thwarts its ritual purpose. For Ahab there is no consummation. Like the hunting priest, he follows the whale forever, accompanied by the sea-hounds, the sharks, who follow his boat on the last day of the chase and pursue him as he is towed behind the whale from the noose made of his own harpoon line.

Ahab sets himself against the current of the informing myths of nature and so destroys himself. But the Ahab impulse, the Puritan impulse, is as natural and inevitable a part of the nature of things as the hunter archetype itself. Ahab Puritanism seems unnatural under the aspect of primitive religion because it violates an ethic which, to the primitive mind, is inherent in nature. Such a judgment is equivalent to Cotton Mather's judgment on the "unnatural" behavior of the Indians, who violated the natural law inherent in the Christian view of the cosmos. Mather delighted in Captain Church's murder of "that great leviathan" Philip, in his history of the Pequot and King Philip wars, but Melville takes no similar delight in the whale's triumph over Ahab. The passion that drives Ahab, as Melville perceives, is as much and as natural a part of the human makeup as its opposite, the spirit that acquiesces in the fulfillment of mythic function.

The cannibals, Indians, islanders, and savages of the *Pequod,* the novice Ishmael, the Quaker Starbuck, the sensual Stubb, and the aggressive Flask are not alternatives to Ahab, as Cotton Mather is to King Philip, but rather specialized extensions of himself. Only Queequeg (and perhaps Mad Pip) stands as a possible alternative. Queequeg respects and loves whales and enjoys a relationship with them that conforms to the fertility mythology. Like Ahab, he bears a king's name and mind. Like Ahab, he is the double of the whale, for the fish is his totem signature and the tatooed sign of kingship that appears on his breast; the tattoos that cover his body are likened to the "hieroglyphics" that marble the skins of whales. Like Ahab he is the agent of the gods, the giver of divine gifts. But where Ahab's deeds or gifts are of death and violence, Queequeg's are of love and kindness. Ahab makes corpses out of the whales; Queequeg, rescuing the Indian Tashtego, dives into the spermy basin of the whale's head to bring a renewed and resurrected life out of that figurative womb. Yet even Queequeg is subordinated to the will of Ahab, not by compulsion after long antagonism but by Ahab's touching of a common chord in the nature of Queequeg as in all his fellows: "My cogged circle fits into all their various wheels, and they revolve."[15] Queequeg's active principle of love, like Starbuck's of dutiful, passive nonaction and Pip's mystical acceptance, is an element of Ahab's character, not an alternative to his character. Ahab himself is the best and fullest expression of the totality of the crew he binds to his will.

In this he is the true American hero, worthy to be captain of a ship whose "wood could only be American,"[16] whose name could only be Indian. Like the American pioneer, he has bound men of God and men of nature, Christians and pagans, captives and captors, Chingachgook and Simon Girty, Boone and Mather, Mary Rowlandson and King Philip within the framework of a single, purposeful endeavor, a quest fraught with complex ironies. Indian and white, materialist and idealist, natural and artificial, passionate and intellectual, stoic and Platonist, Prometheus and Faust have all been amalgamated in a single vessel, bound into the wilderness of the world and of the human mind, to seek out and murder the very spirit and essence of world, mind, and wilderness.

For it is the essence of the real that Ahab seeks to destroy, devour, assimilate to himself, replace with his own being and intelligence. He speaks always of a "reasoning thing," a thing therefore like himself, behind the mask that is Moby Dick, behind the veil that hides the true face of nature's god. "Moby" Dick's name may refer us to Hamlet's Gertrude, the masked or "mobled Queen" (II.ii.506-8), who seems a loving wife and mother and may be a murderous jade. Yet, as Pip's vision tells us, this reasoning thing may be merely the wish of maddened Ahab, not a true vision: for the God that Pip beholds is "indifferent," insentient, compacted of an infinitude of deaths, just as the "orbs" or islands of the ocean are fabrications of the meaningless, redundant, undifferentiated, time-extended deaths of billions of "coral insects"— which is to say that God is indistinguishable from the nonhuman,

[15]Ibid., p. 166.
[16]Ibid., p. 564.

unreasoning processes of the world-as-it-is. When Ahab confronts that reality in the blank forehead of the faceless whale, he and his ship are cracked like lice, or like bodies fallen at random into the heart of a huge dynamo. Ahab's Promethean-Satanic dreams and all the individuated existences so carefully accumulated in the foregoing chapters drop in a moment into the shapeless maw of the undifferentiating sea. The whale swims off, marked a bit more with obscure hieroglyphics, but with no recognition or memory of his victims' peculiar aims and identities. "Then all collapsed, and the great shroud of the sea rolled on as it rolled five thousand years ago." Nothing has changed of the eternal, divine processes of the world; but all that man has been here has collapsed, vanished in an apocalyptic holocaust, leaving only one mind to remember and carry the tale to us.

The Image of Society in *Moby-Dick*

by Henry Nash Smith

In the most obvious and literal sense, the material of *Moby-Dick* is drawn directly from nineteenth-century American society. The narrative framework is provided by a whaling cruise. The author takes pains to report technical facts accurately. The ostensible motivations of the principal characters have to do with the conduct of this economic enterprise. And the book grows out of American experience in yet richer and deeper ways. Richard Chase, for example, has pointed out Melville's debt to American folklore, his preoccupation with such characteristic American phenomena as Transcendentalism and humanitarian crusades, his interest in the West. These elements in the novel register the effects of energies flowing from the society through the imagination of the author into his work.

The most conspicuous result of this influence on the novel is its abundant metaphorical material. Melville makes especially wide and various use of allusions to the West and to the machine. In chapter xlii ("The Whiteness of the Whale"), for example, his allusions to the White Steed of the Prairies and the musky scent of a buffalo robe from Oregon show that the blank wilderness of the Far West had for him varied and intense meanings. The images suggest imperial, even archangelical majesty, primeval innocence, and at the same time "the demonism of the world." These emotions are built into the attitude we are meant to have toward the White Whale through one of the most complicated figurative maneuvers in American literature. Similarly, as the final chase rises to its climax, Ahab's power to dispel the "pale fears and

"The Image of Society in *Moby-Dick*" by Henry Nash Smith. From *Moby-Dick: Centennial Essays,* edited by Tyrus Hillway and Luther S. Mansfield (Dallas: Southern Methodist University Press, 1953), pp. 59-75. Copyright 1953 by Southern Methodist University Press. Reprinted by permission of the publisher.

forebodings of the crew" is compared to the effect of a "bounding bison" on timid prairie hares.

Ahab is likewise endowed with menacing and irresistible force through being associated with the machines of the Industrial Revolution. There are a number of passages in *Moby-Dick* indicating that Melville felt an almost physical apprehension toward the machine. Thus in chapter lx ("The Line") we read: "For, when the line is darting out, to be seated then in the boat, is like being seated in the midst of the manifold whizzings of a steam-engine in full play, when every flying beam, and shaft, and wheel, is grazing you." Melville exploits this ominous character of the machine in chapter xxxvii ("Sunset") to express Ahab's inhuman determination to use the crew of the *Pequod* as mere tools. Ahab feels that he wears an iron crown; he lacks "the low, enjoying power" of ordinary human beings. "I thought to find one stubborn," he says, "at the least; but my one cogged circle fits into all their various wheels, and they revolve." And in the often-quoted conclusion of the chapter, he exclaims to the "great gods":

> Swerve me? ye cannot swerve me, else you swerve yourselves! man has ye there. Swerve me? The path to my fixed purpose is laid with iron rails, whereon my soul is grooved to run. Over unsounded gorges, through the rifled hearts of mountains, under torrents' beds, unerringly I rush! Naught's an obstacle, naught's an angle to the iron way!

At the beginning of the next chapter Melville gives to Starbuck an image from mining to stand beside the railroad image: Ahab "drilled deep down, and blasted all my reason out of me!"

The general impression conveyed here is that machines violate humanity. The one other passage of considerable length in which technology is drawn upon is more ambiguous, so complex indeed that it almost defies exegesis. It concerns the whale's skeleton in "A Bower in the Arsacides" (chapter cii):

> The wood was green as mosses of the Icy Glen; the trees stood high and haughty, feeling their living sap; the industrious earth beneath was as a weaver's loom, with a gorgeous carpet on it, whereof the ground-vine tendrils formed the warp and woof, and the living flowers the figures. All the trees, with all their laden branches; all the shrubs, and ferns, and grasses; the message-carrying air; all these unceasingly were active. Through the lacings of the leaves,

the great sun seemed a flying shuttle weaving the unwearied verdure. Oh, busy weaver! unseen weaver!—pause!—one word!—
whither flows the fabric? what palace may it deck? wherefore all
these ceaseless toilings? Speak, weaver!—stay thy hand!—but one
single word with thee! Nay—the shuttle flies—the figures float from
forth the loom; the freshet-rushing carpet for ever slides away. The
weaver-god, he weaves; and by that weaving is he deafened, that he
hears no mortal voice; and by that humming, we, too, who look on
the loom are deafened; and only when we escape it shall we hear the
thousand voices that speak through it. For even so is it in all material factories. The spoken words that are inaudible among the flying
spindles; those same spoken words are plainly heard without the
walls, bursting from the opened casements. Thereby have villainies
been detected. Ah, mortal! then, be heedful; for so, in all this din of
the great world's loom, thy subtlest thinkings may be overheard afar.

   Now, amid the green, life-restless loom of that Arsacidean wood,
the great, white, worshipped skeleton lay lounging—a gigantic
idler! Yet, as the ever-woven verdant warp and woof intermixed
and hummed around him, the mighty idler seemed the cunning
weaver; himself all woven over with the vines; every month assum-
ing greener, fresher verdure; but himself a skeleton. Life folded
Death; Death trellised Life, the grim god wived with youthful Life,
and begat him curly-headed glories.

There are a number of difficulties in the passage. The role of the
sun, for example, is confusing. As weaver-god the sun tends to
be personified, and he is anthropomorphic enough to be deafened;
but the sun is also a flying shuttle, and the act of weaving seems
sometimes that of a person tending a loom, sometimes the action of
the loom itself. The skeleton of the whale is inactive yet also seems
engaged in weaving; it is Death yet also a god capable of begetting
offspring. Chapter xlvii ("The Mat-Maker") has prepared us to see
in the process of weaving a complex analogical statement concerning fate, free will, and chance; this implication is present here also,
and the skeleton-loom takes on some of the character of fate. But
at the end of the chapter, in the position where Melville ordinarily
develops his important symbolic inferences, the warning that our
thoughts may be overheard seems odd and trivial after the grave
suggestions that have been thrown out immediately before, and it
is not congruous with the remarks concerning Death and Life that
immediately follow. The vital activity of the plants merges indis-
tinguishably with the mechanical activity of the loom, so that the
machine does not seem here to be an inorganic menace to life. And

since the tone of the chapter is playful on the whole, we are restrained from giving to these cosmic materials the weight they
might have in a different setting.

The difficulties presented by "A Bower in the Arsacides" are
highly suggestive. The chapter provides abundant evidence that
industrialism and technology had made a deep impression on
Melville: he associates images drawn from this source with ideas
of the greatest moment. But the material is not fully worked out;
its meaning seems to be urgent, yet is not brought to formal
clarity. The industrial imagery associated with Ahab is more
consistent. It is always malign in implication, and its cumulative
effect lends to him an impressive strength. This imagery has
seemed to support the interpretation of Ahab as an embodiment
of the inhuman will-to-power which Melville discerned in developing American capitalism. Yet I do not think that the industrial imagery, taken as a whole, provides, or was meant to provide,
a coherent image of American society. I should like to inquire
whether *Moby-Dick* contains such an image. To some extent this
is to ask whether the subject matter of the science of sociology
was present as an identifiable concept to Melville's mind. Such
an inquiry might seem trivial, but it is not necessarily so; for it is
the basis for raising the further question of whether society
functions as an entity in the action of the book. And in a work of
art, *Esse est percipi.*

The opening pages of *Moby-Dick* make it plain that Melville
was intensely interested in at least one problem which involves
"society" as we understand it — the problem of alienation, of disturbance in the relation between the individual and the community. To choose the name Ishmael for his narrator was to
designate this relation as a primary theme of the novel. The name
and the biblical story which it called up were often mentioned by
American writers in the early nineteenth century. The figure of
the outcast was fascinating to a society whose official code of
values gave an especially high value to conformity — whether the
outcast was felt to be elegantly misanthropic, like Childe Harold,
or strong but crude and barbaric, like the frontiersman Ishmael
Bush in Cooper's *The Prairie*. A great deal of attention was paid
to the Bedouin Arabs, for example, and to the wild Indians of the
Great Plains, both groups being recognized as "Ishmaelites." The
migratory life of these nomads of the desert was habitually con-
trasted with the "social state" of people who lived by agriculture

and possessed settled places of abode. The contrast was felt to raise the basic issue of the rationale of society, the issue of primitivism.

Such considerations were evidently present to Melville when he chose to convey the events of his story through the mind of a fugitive from society, a man alienated from the normal life of settled communities. Ishmael has no stake in society: he is penniless and apparently without relatives. His "splintered heart and maddened hand were turned against the wolfish world." Feeling as he does, he might kill himself, as Cato did; instead, he escapes to the unsocial wastes of the sea.

Ishmael is an American, and he ships on the *Pequod* in Nantucket harbor. In a vague sense, therefore, the wolfish world from which he is fleeing is an American world. But Melville does not insist on this, and Ishmael's case against society is general rather than specific. What we have in the opening chapters is a hostility toward all social institutions rather than a specific indictment of American society. The Nineveh of Father Mapple's sermon is just as relevant as New York to Ishmael's and the author's meaning. The problem, indeed, tends to become more rather than less abstract and generalized. We hear, for example, the "mortally intolerable truth; that all deep, earnest thinking is but the intrepid effort of the soul to keep the open independence of her sea; while the wildest winds of heaven and earth conspire to cast her on the treacherous, slavish shore." Ishmael's admiration for "deep, earnest thinking" and for the independence of the soul requires us to see a close parallel between him and the Jonah who was divinely appointed to be a "pilot-prophet, or speaker of true things." And Melville evidently agrees with the stirring exhortation of Father Mapple:

> Delight is to him—a far, far upward and inward delight—who against the proud gods and commodores of this earth, ever stands forth his own inexorable self. Delight is to him whose strong arms yet support him, when the ship of this base treacherous world has gone down beneath him. Delight is to him, who gives no quarter in the truth, and kills, burns, and destroys all sin though he pluck it out from under the robes of Senators and Judges.

The sentiments with which Ishmael shipped on the *Pequod,* and those developed in Father Mapple's sermon, derive from the assumption that organized society is intrinsically evil. Despite the pretense of virtue that characterizes official codes of morals, society is founded on force and fraud. Its rulers—the proud commodores, the senators and judges—are but the more eminent in wickedness and in hypocrisy. They are the mighty ones whom every speaker of truth, every Jonah sent to preach to wicked Nineveh, must defy. Every anointed prophet of the Lord will become an outcast driven forth for the crime of uttering the truth.

It is evident that from such a standpoint Melville can develop no sanction for the institutions of organized society. The state and political theories, the law, property rights—none has ethical standing; all are expressions of force, thinly masked by fraud. The most extensive passage embodying such a judgment of social institutions is in chapter lxxxix ("Fast-Fish and Loose-Fish"). After a brief allusion to the British law of whale-trover, Melville concludes that "these two laws touching Fast-Fish and Loose-Fish ...will, on reflection, be found the fundamentals of all human jurisprudence; for notwithstanding its complicated tracery of sculpture, the Temple of the Law, like the Temple of the Philistines, has but two props to stand on." The succeeding paragraphs itemize many aspects of the institutionalized behavior of men and of nations, all by implication unjust, all sustained, according to the way of the world, by force: serfdom in Russia and slavery in the United States; the rent collected by the rapacious landlord from the poor widow; the "undetected villain's marble mansion with a doorplate for a waif"; the ruinous interest demanded of "poor Woebegone, the bankrupt, on a loan to keep Woebegone's family from starvation"; the Archbishop of Savesoul's £100,000 of income, "seized from the scant bread and cheese of hundreds of thousands of broken-backed laborers." The radical accusation of unjust force is further applied to England's control of Ireland and India, the seizure of Texas (and eventually of all Mexico) by the United States, of America by Spain in 1492, of Poland by the Czar, of Greece by the Turks. The denial of any moral basis for political institutions is finally carried to the utmost extremity: "What are the Rights of Man and the Liberties of the World but Loose-Fish? What all men's minds and opinions but Loose-Fish?"

To the extent that these passages embody a political theory, I do not see how it can be described as anything except philosophical anarchy, with the strong overtones of primitivism that philosophical anarchy usually has. Not only are political and

economic forms wicked: they are irredeemable. It does not occur
to Melville that institutions might be improved. He has nothing
in common with the social reformer. The only course open to a
man of insight and courage is to denounce the wolfish world
though he should die for it.

If we turn from explicit assertions to indirect propositions
conveyed by symbols, we discover other implications of the same
general tenor. Melville's principal symbol here is the sharks
(closely associated with swordfish and other formidable monsters
of the deep). I should like to notice the sharks in several passages
from different portions of the novel. The most extended treatment of them is the episode of Fleece's sermon, in chapter lxiv
("Stubb's Supper"). In the introduction to this scene the undersea
world of the sharks is said to be an exact duplicate of the "smoking
horror and diabolism of a sea-fight"; it suggests "the propriety of
devil-worship, and the expediency of conciliating the devil."
Presently the sharks tearing mouthfuls of flesh from the dead
whale become a congregation of "Belubed fellow-critters" to
whom the minister addresses a discourse on the nature of man:
"...if you gobern de shark in you, why den you be angel; for all
angel is not'ing more dan de shark well goberned." But the main
point of the passage concerns economic justice: no member of a
society has a right to a larger share of the available resources than
any other member (after all, the whale they are eating belongs to
someone else). Some have big mouths, some small; "so dat de
brigness ob de mout is not to swaller wid, but to bite off de blubber for de small fry ob sharks, dat can't get into de scrouge to
help demselves." The economic order of a competitive society is,
then, a "scrouge." Nevertheless, individuals with a competitive
advantage have the obligation of stewardship, to share their gains
with the less successful. "That's Christianity," cries Stubb; but
Fleece knows it is futile to preach such a doctrine:

> No use goin' on; de dam willains will keep a scrougin' and slappin'
> each oder, Massa Stubb; dey don't hear one word; no use a-preaching
> to such dam g'uttons as you call 'em, till dare bellies is full, and dare
> bellies is bottomless; and when dey do get 'em full, dey won't hear
> you den; for den dey sink in de sea, go fast to sleep on de coral, and
> can't hear not'ing at all, for eber and eber.

The image of human society presented here is familiar in the
history of political thought, from ancient times (*"Homo homini*

lupus") to the theory of twentieth-century naturalism, as in the celebrated passage about the lobster and the squid near the beginning of Dreiser's *The Financier*. With the exception of one brief passage in the Epilogue, which will be discussed later, Melville's sharks always have the same role, and they appear in two later passages of considerable length—in chapter cxiv ("The Gilder") and chapter cxxxii ("The Symphony"). These chapters, however, introduce complexities of meaning which require additional comment. In both, the sharks are still cruel and sinister. But the evil they symbolize has ceased to be primarily economic. The sharks have become an adumbration of the "invisible spheres" which we know were "formed in fright." A symbol which has appeared earlier as a commentary on society now takes on a much wider range of reference, and we are faced with the question of how much social content it still retains. Furthermore, in both the late chapters the sharks and their habitat the sea do not fill the picture but are carefully shown in contrast with a bland, peaceful upper air. I should like to examine these two passages at some length in order to determine whether Melville's use of the sharks in a larger symbolic scheme expresses any of his thought about society.

Chapter cxiv ("The Gilder") follows immediately after the chapter entitled "The Forge," with its climax in the blasphemous parody of the baptismal service as Ahab plunges his new-forged harpoon into the blood of the harpooners. Melville throws his Gothic diabolism into relief by a chapter restating the minor theme of pastoral quiet:

> At such times, under an abated sun; afloat all day upon smooth, slow heaving swells; seated in his boat, light as a birch canoe; and so sociably mixing with the soft waves themselves, that like hearthstone cats they purr against the gunwale; these are the times of dreamy quietude, when beholding the tranquil beauty and brilliance of the ocean's skin, one forgets the tiger heart that pants beneath it; and would not willingly remember, that this velvet paw but conceals a remorseless fang.
>
> These are the times, when in his whale-boat the rover softly feels a certain filial, confident, land-like feeling towards the sea; that he regards it as so much flowery earth; and the distant ship revealing only the tops of her masts, seems struggling forward, not through highly rolling waves, but through the tall grass of a rolling prairie: as when the western emigrants' horses only show their erected ears, while their hidden bodies widely wade through the amazing verdure.

The long-drawn virgin vales; the mild blue hill-sides; as over these there steals the hush, the hum; you almost swear that play-wearied children lie sleeping in these solitudes, in some glad May-time, when the flowers of the woods are plucked. And all this mixes with your most mystic mood; so that fact and fancy, half-way meeting, interpenetrate, and form one seamless whole. ...
Oh, grassy glades! oh, ever vernal endless landscapes in the soul; in ye,—though long parched by the dead drought of the earthy life,—in ye, men may yet roll, like young horses in new morning clover; and for some few fleeting moments, feel the cool dew of the life immortal on them. Would to God these blessed calms would last. But the mingled, mingling threads of life are woven by warp and woof: calms crossed by storms, a storm for every calm. ... Where lies the final harbor, whence we unmoor no more? In what rapt ether sails the world, of which the weariest will never weary? Where is the foundling's father hidden? Our souls are like those orphans whose unwedded mothers die in bearing them: the secret of our paternity lies in their grave, and we must there to learn it.
And that same day, too, gazing far down from his boat's side into that same golden sea, Starbuck slowly murmured: —
"Loveliness unfathomable, as ever lover saw in his young bride's eye!—Tell me not of thy teeth-tiered sharks, and thy kidnapping cannibal ways. Let faith oust fact; let fancy oust memory; I look deep down and do believe."

In this passage, the teeth-tiered sharks are given the status of fact. The evil depths of the ocean are the reality about which the structure is built. This evil is, momentarily, concealed beneath the tranquil beauty of the ocean's skin, the golden surface of pastoral peace, with its associations of flowery earth, the found parents of the orphan, the sleeping children in May-time, the loveliness which the lover sees in the young bride's eye. But this "cool dew of the life immortal" is quite unreal. Only when faith ousts fact, when fancy ousts memory can Starbuck look deep down and believe, and the secret of our paternity will be revealed only in the grave.
A similar pattern of meaning is established a little later, on the eve of the final chase of the white whale, when the *Pequod* encounters the ironically named *Delight* engaged in burying the only one of five men killed by the whale whose body has been recovered:

The firmaments of air and sea were hardly separable in that all-pervading azure; only, the pensive air was transparently pure and

soft, with a woman's look, and the robust and man-like sea heaved
with long, strong, lingering swells, as Samson's chest in his sleep.

Hither, and thither, on high, glided the snow-white wings of
small, unspeckled birds; these were the gentle thoughts of
the feminine air; but to and fro in the deeps, far down in the bottomless blue, rushed mighty leviathans, sword-fish, and sharks; and
these were the strong, troubled, murderous thinkings of the masculine sea.

But though thus contrasting within, the contrast was only in
shades and shadows without; those two seemed one; it was only
the sex, as it were, that distinguished them.

The feminine character of the gentle sky is developed in the
remainder of the chapter, as Ahab recalls his wife and child, but
acknowledges his bondage to some "nameless, inscrutable, un-
earthly thing," some "cozening, hidden lord and master" that
compels him to the fatal quest.

What is the meaning of this twice-developed contrast between a
bland, peaceful, feminine upper air, and the murderous masculine depths of the ocean? The air is explicitly labeled mere appearance; yet it is associated with the images of wife and child as
well as with that of traitorous Delilah. The ocean depths are
characterized as real; yet they conceal the hideous force which is
presently to sink the *Pequod,* destroy captain and crew, and leave
only Ishmael alive to tell the tale. We recognize many more implications in the sharks than they had in the scene of Fleece's
sermon. Yet we can hardly suppose there is no connection between
the earlier appearance of the sharks and their function here. While
I do not feel confident that I understand fully what is going on in
the latter passages, I suggest that there is some submerged allusion
to Melville's conception of society in them. He has several times
hinted at an association between the peaceful upper air and what
might be called the superstructure of society—the realm of fantasy, of revery, of transcendental speculation. Howard Vincent
has called attention to the way in which Melville has adapted a
passage from J. Ross Browne's *Etchings of a Whaling Cruise*
about standing mastheads. Browne's description of the "little
world of peace and seclusion, where I could think over past times
without interruption" and of the "vague and visionary fancies"
which occupied him on such occasions, until he was rudely awakened by the captain's shouted warning to "keep a sharp lookout
for whales," strongly suggests a contrast between the realities of

the whaling cruise and the private world of revery and memories of the past. Browne's rather stilted allusion to "those ethereal and refined fancies which Rousseau has so beautifully described as part of the inspiration derived from an elevated atmosphere," and particularly his repeated statement that the reveries at the masthead were mainly "dreams of home," throw a good deal of light on Melville's use of the materials. Melville calls the dreamer a "sunken-eyed young Platonist" and suggests a situation not unlike his own and Ishmael's aboard the whaler:

> ...nowadays, the whale-fishery furnishes an asylum for many romantic, melancholy, and absent-minded young men, disgusted with the carking care of earth, and seeking sentiment in tar and blubber. Childe Harold not unfrequently perches himself upon the mast-head of some luckless disappointed whale-ship, and in moody phase ejaculates: —
> "Roll on, thou deep and dark blue ocean, roll!
> Ten thousand blubber-hunters sweep over thee in vain."

And while identifying himself to a considerable extent with Browne and with the other young sunken-eyed Platonists, Melville yet phrases a warning to himself and to them:

> ...lulled into such an opium-like listlessness of vacant, unconscious reverie is this absent-minded youth by the blending cadence of waves with thoughts, that at last he loses his identity; takes the mystic ocean at his feet for the visible image of that deep, blue, bottomless soul, pervading mankind and nature; and every strange, half-seen, gliding, beautiful thing that eludes him; every dimly-discovered, uprising fin of some undiscernible form, seems to him the embodiment of those elusive thoughts that only people the soul by continually flitting through it. In this enchanted mood, thy spirit ebbs away to whence it came; becomes diffused through time and space; like Cranmer's sprinkled Pantheistic ashes, forming at last a part of every shore the round globe over.
> There is no life in thee, now, excepting that rocking life imparted by a gentle rolling ship; by her, borrowed from the sea; by the sea, from the inscrutable tides of God. But while this sleep, this dream is on ye, move your foot or hand an inch; slip your hold at all; and your identity comes back in horror. Over Descartian vortices you hover. And perhaps, at mid-day, in the fairest weather, with one half-throttled shriek you drop through that transparent air into the summer sea, no more to rise for ever. Heed it well, ye Pantheists!

Without pretending to do justice to all the nuances of implication here, I think we can nevertheless recognize that the sea is
the realm of Descartian vortices, the realm of mindless matter,
or of equally mindless institutions. Mr. Vincent glosses the phrase
(with reference to a similar allusion in *Pierre*) as "the brute,
material (and often evil) facts of life." It is a dangerous delusion
to imagine that the dimly discovered forms observed beneath the
surface are harmless fantasies; they are the teeth-tiered sharks,
and he who falls into the ocean with a half-throttled shriek will
rise no more for ever. The upper air of Pantheistic revery is, of
course, in some vague sense transcendental speculation, for which
Melville confesses a weakness, but which he consistently condemns. The realm of the upper air, unreal, deceptive, and feminine, is associated with Rousseau and Byron. It is, in a word, the
sphere of what Melville's contemporaries called "ideality," the
genteel official culture of the 1830's and 1840's. I suggest therefore that "The Gilder" and "The Symphony" present an image oɪ
society having two aspects: a substratum of rapacious competition,
with a tiger heart, the sphere of masculine murderous sharks and
leviathans; and a fictitious, aerial superstructure of peace, beauty,
revery, poetry, feminine in tone, passive not active, delightful
but deceptive, as Delilah was deceptive. Melville feels sympathy
with both these spheres. He is led by temperament to dream in a
languid fashion not unlike Browne's, just as in *Mardi* he could
take a now incomprehensible pleasure in the language of flowers.
He is likewise powerfully attracted by "the overwhelming idea of
the great whale himself," which is archangelical and kingly in its
majesty even in the act of destruction. In the end, however, he
can accept neither—the beautiful feminine air is false, the murderous sea is ruthless.

But is it true that *Moby-Dick* affirms no social values whatever? To say this would evidently be an exaggeration. Here the
final appearance of the sharks is suggestive. In the Epilogue we
read:

> Buoyed up by that coffin, for almost one whole day and night, I
> floated on a soft and dirge-like main. The unharming sharks, they
> glided by as if with padlocks on their mouths; the savage sea-hawks
> sailed with sheathed beaks. On the second day, a sail drew near,
> nearer, and picked me up at last. It was the devious-cruising Rachel,
> that in her retracing search after her missing children, only found
> another orphan.

Something has happened to the sharks. I am not sure exactly what; there is a hint of supernatural force applied to restrain them for Ishmael's express benefit, perhaps in token of his salvation or resurrection. In any event, the splintered heart and maddened hand have been transformed by the action of the novel; and while we are not told explicitly that Ishmael is reconciled to a wolfish world which had once seemed to him unalterably malign, the tone of the ending suggests peace and reconciliation. We are therefore led to inquire into the affirmations, the positive forces which have been revealed in the course of the action. Unless we can discover what these are, Ishmael's survival is meaningless.

It seems to me that no affirmations in the novel extend to "the world," as a whole. As has been remarked above, there is no evidence that society can be redeemed, or that institutions once regarded as wicked are later discovered to be otherwise. Melville's procedure is rather to single out certain experiences within the larger field of social relationships which can be affirmed and from which durable values can be derived. If society is evil, some human relationships are nevertheless good. These can be designated by the general name of brotherhood or community, and Ishmael's love for Queequeg is the most obvious example of a redeeming force brought to bear upon him in the course of action. This love exists between two men who are, so to speak, outside society— Ishmael by choice, Queequeg by birth. But to the extent that they can cherish one another they escape from the dreadful fate of being "isolatoes," discrete individuals without the sustenance of membership in a human community. Men can be saved although society is damned. From his intense personal relationship with Queequeg, Ishmael eventually broadens his capacity for comradeship to include the crew as a whole. The key passage here is, of course, the end of chapter xxvi ("Knights and Squires") on the "immaculate manliness" and "democratic dignity" of "man, in the ideal" which endures despite the fact that "men may seem detestable, as joint stock companies and nations." This august dignity is the central affirmation of the novel. But it is not primarily a social value at all. The democracy which Melville has in mind is not a political system or even a social system. It is independent of institutions. Like Emerson's Self-Reliance, it is sustained by a transaction between the individual and the great democratic God, the "just spirit of Equality, which [has] spread one royal mantle of humanity over all my kind!"

By a slight extension of the theme of brotherhood, of love between man and man, Melville includes the everyday satisfactions
of family life—again without reference to anything so abstract
as society or institutions:

> For now, since by many prolonged, repeated experiences, I have
> perceived that in all cases man must eventually lower, or at least
> shift, his conceit of attainable felicity; not placing it anywhere in
> the intellect or the fancy; but in the wife, the heart, the bed, the ta-
> ble, the saddle, the fireside, the country; now that I have perceived
> all this, I am ready to squeeze case eternally.

Wife and child—Starbuck's and Ahab's—are likewise given the
status of strongly affirmative symbols in "The Symphony," just
before the catastrophe of the final chase, although even "the
lovely aromas in that enchanted air" were unable, for more than
a moment, to "dispel...the cantankerous thing" in Ahab's soul.
   This short list seems to me to include all the important affirmations in the novel that bear upon Ishmael's original alienation from the world. Here, if anywhere, must we find the force
that draws him back from suicide or flight into the desert, and
reconciles him to life and, by implication, to society. I suggest
that this centrally important process is not adequately worked out
in the novel, that Ishmael's catharsis—which, we cannot help
feeling, to a marked degree embodies Melville's—is not sufficiently
specified. At the end of the book, we are convinced it has occurred,
but we are not fully able to say how or why. Ishmael's survival is
thus to a considerable extent miraculous. In a universe without God,
such a miracle is hard to account for.
   If I may now return to the question raised at the beginning of the
paper, I think this examination of *Moby-Dick* leads to the conclusion not only that the central social problem in the novel is
alienation, but that alienation is the central theme of the book as
a whole. This view makes Ishmael rather than Ahab the "hero,"
and relegates the quest of the White Whale to a subordinate position in the basic structure of the narrative. Ahab, from this standpoint, can be taken as an exemplification of any of a number of
wrong and dangerous attitudes—for our present purposes we are
not obliged to decide which. Ishmael is tending toward a similar
condition at the opening of the story, and Ahab certainly embodies on a grander scale impulses which Ishmael and Melville
feel within themselves. Ishmael is consequently drawn into the

orbit of Ahab's morbid and wicked undertaking, but he finally escapes and survives. We are meant to believe that he survives because the splintered heart and maddened hand have somehow been healed. And even though Melville is unable to provide us with a fully specified resolution of his problem, his book forces us to recognize that for him, at least, American society of the mid-nineteenth century represented not the benign present and hopeful future proclaimed by official spokesmen, but an environment threatening the individual with a disintegration of personality which he could avoid only by the half-miraculous achievement of a sense of community, of brotherhood, unattainable within the official culture—a sense of community to be found, in fact, only among "meanest mariners, and renegades and castaways."

Moby-Dick

by Richard B. Sewall

It is easy to see why Melville, himself a prey to the deepest forebodings about the optimism of his day, recognized at once his kinship of spirit with Hawthorne. "There is a certain tragic phase of humanity which, in our opinion [he wrote], was never more powerfully embodied than by Hawthorne."[1] A year after Hawthorne published *The Scarlet Letter,* Melville dedicated his own most powerful embodiment of this tragic phase, *Moby-Dick,* to Hawthorne, his acknowledged master. Together the two books are witness to the vitality of the tragic vision, which pierces beneath the "official view" of any culture to the dark realities that can never be permanently hidden,[2] and together they mark a recrudescence of the tragic spirit in what would seem an unlikely time, on unlikely soil, and without benefit of tragic theater or tragic audience. Both authors were aware of the untimeliness of their books.

From *The Vision of Tragedy,* by Richard B. Sewall (New Haven, Conn.: Yale University Press, 1959), pp. 92-105. Copyright © 1959 by Yale University Press. Reprinted by permission of the publisher.

[1]F. O. Matthiessen quotes this remark early in his discussion of Hawthorne *(American Renaissance* [New York, Oxford University Press, 1941], p. 192). His account of the literary affinities between Hawthorne and Melville includes much that is true not only of their place in mid-nineteenth-century America but in the tragic tradition in general. See especially the opening paragraphs of his chapter, "The Vision of Evil" (pp. 179-80). Later (p. 189) he says that it was Melville's meditation on Shakespeare that "brought him to his first profound comprehension of the nature of tragedy." What Melville liked in Hawthorne, writes Matthiessen, was "the same kind of 'short, quick probings at the very axis of reality' that had so impressed him in Shakespeare."

[2]In *The Melville Log,* ed. Jay Leyda (New York, Harcourt, Brace, 1951), there is the following entry under March 23, 1850 *(Moby-Dick* was begun Feb. 1, 1850): "M. acquires another Bible....In *Job* ...Chapter 13 he scores and underscores: 15 Though he slay me, yet will I trust in him: *but I will maintain mine own ways before him."* My attention was called to this entry by Laurence Michel.

Hawthorne, in the famous letter to his publisher, Fields, spoke of fearing that his novel would "weary very many people and disgust some" by keeping so close, and with so little diversification, to "the same dark idea." Would he have an audience receptive to his peculiar view of things? The Greek and Elizabethan dramatists or Racine or even the Poet of Job could count on an audience culturally predisposed through myth, theater, or racial view to accept at once a drama of direness. Hawthorne had to make his own audience, to lead it by easy stages, as it were, into the dark idea. Hence the familiar, reassuring tone of the Custom House introduction, where the only dire events involve a certain goose of tragic toughness and the routine political loss of a job not worth holding. Hence the whimsical apology, in advance, for the "stern and sombre aspect" of Hester's story—"too much ungladdened by genial sunshine; too little relieved by the tender and familiar influences which soften almost every scene of nature and real life, and, undoubtedly, should soften every picture of them" —an apology which we may well regard as almost wholly tactical.

And hence (among other reasons) the long preliminary phase of *Moby-Dick,* introducing Ishmael, the reassuringly normal one who would go to sea now and again to drive off the spleen, or merely to satisfy "an everlasting itch for things remote"; who would take "the universal thump" with equanimity, and cry three cheers for Nantucket—"and come a stove boat and stove body when they will, for stave my soul, Jove himself cannot." The world of Ishmael's setting forth, like the world of the Custom House, was undimmed by the dark idea and seemingly invulnerable to any Jovian thunderbolts. God was above young Ishmael's world as he packed his bag for Cape Horn and the Pacific; and even as he read on the tablets of Father Mapple's chapel in New Bedford the fate of the whalemen who had gone before him, he "grew merry again." The rest of his story shows how shallow his optimism was, as Melville leads him (and the untragic American audience) by slow degrees, but remorselessly, toward tragic truth.

Ishmael has been called the chorus to Ahab as tragic hero, but this is hardly adequate to describe his total participation in the tragic action. To be sure, the Aeschylean choruses became involved, acted, and suffered as the other choruses in Greek drama for the most part did not. But it is significant of Melville's task of rendering his tragedy probable to his age that Ishmael frames and

pervades the story as no Greek chorus does. He is a constant link
to the known and familiar. He is average, goodhearted humanity,
though somewhat more given to meditation than most and (as he
says of himself) "quick to perceive a horror." His optimism lies
not in his denial that the horror is there but in his hope of being
"social with it"—"since it is but well to be on friendly terms with
all the inmates of the place one lodges in." Only gradually does
this hope come to be fully tested. All the little horrors of the early
stages of his adventures are accommodated to his hearty, comic
vision. He accepts the wintry and forbidding conditions of his
stay in New Bedford with good cheer. The inauspicious omens in
Father Mapple's chapel fail to daunt him. He shares his bed with
the terrifying Queequeg, and rejoices in the evidence of natural
goodness even in this pagan cannibal. Queequeg's rescue of the
man overboard on the trip to Nantucket confirms his faith in his
new friend and in this "mutual joint-stock world" where Christians and cannibals live and let live. "Dost know nothing at all
about whaling, I dare say—eh?" asks Captain Peleg as Ishmael
presents himself at the *Pequod* to sign on for the voyage. "Nothing,
Sir," he answers handsomely; "but I have no doubt I shall soon
learn." Only Peleg's strange confidences about the captain of the
Pequod—that "grand, ungodly, god-like man, Captain Ahab"—
momentarily shake his confidence that there is no horror he cannot be social with. As he hears the story of Ahab's fierce troubles,
he is filled "with a certain wild vagueness of painfulness concerning him"—"a sympathy and a sorrow for him, but for I don't
know what, unless it was the cruel loss of his leg." But more than
that—"a strange awe of him; but that sort of awe, which I cannot at
all describe, was not exactly awe; I do not know what it was."

Such were the first intimations to this young novitiate of mysteries not to be resolved by his philosophy, the first hint (as
Stephen Daedalus was later to refine on Aristotle's notion of
terror) of "the feeling which arrests the mind in the presence of
whatsoever is grave and constant in human sufferings and unites
it with the secret cause." So far in Ishmael's experience whatever
had been grave had not been constant, and what had been constant had not been grave. Pity, of the sort which he felt for Ahab's
misfortune, is a passing thing, as he soon confesses: "However, my
thoughts were at length carried in other directions, so that for the
present dark Ahab slipped my mind."

But the sense of awe, the intimations of terror, were not to be denied, nor the full terror in store. Queequeg's pagan fanaticisms, his all-day Ramadan, or Fasting and Humiliation, were easy for Ishmael's ready rationalism—"I say, we good Presbyterian Christians should be charitable in these things, and not fancy ourselves so vastly superior to other mortals, pagans and what not, because of their half-crazy conceits on these subjects"—and he pled with his cannibal friend to give over his "prolonged ham-squattings in cold, cheerless rooms" as opposed to "the obvious laws of Hygiene and common sense." But he could not so easily accommodate his second warning about Ahab, this time from old Elijah, whose "ambiguous, half-hinting, half-revealing, shrouded sort of talk begat in me all kinds of vague wonderments and half-apprehensions." He even chided himself for not facing squarely this challenge to his security, but in the busy preparations for the voyage he "said nothing, and tried to think nothing." In such situations, he said, a man "insensibly strives to cover up his suspicions even from himself."

But in spite of himself he was coming ever nearer the vortex. One morning, several days out, "as I levelled my glance toward the taffrail, foreboding shivers ran over me. Reality outran apprehension; Captain Ahab stood upon his quarter-deck." What Ishmael saw for the first time was no Queequeg with his crazy conceits, nor "humbug" Elijah, but a man "with a crucifixion in his face," standing there "in all the nameless regal overbearing dignity of some mighty woe." Ahab had looked on terror, and Ishmael looked on Ahab. Soon he was to stare into it face to face.

Somewhat before this first startling encounter, Melville had begun to shift his method from the narrative mode to the dramatic. It is as if he were confident by now that the bridge was whole and firm between the world of his readers and the tragic world of his imaginings. Ishmael was doing his work; the audience, like him, is almost ready for the full revelation. The "Knights and Squires" of the ship's company have been introduced. Stubb has had his first encounter with Ahab, told not by Ishmael but by Melville as dramatist: Stubb's mild plea that Ahab curtail his nightly deck-walks over the sleeping sailors' heads; Ahab's furious rebuke: "Down, dog, and kennel"; and Stubb's bewildered ruminations: "He's full of riddles.... Damn me, but all things are queer, come to think of 'em." We have met the staid and steadfast Starbuck,

"firm in the conflict with seas, or winds, or whales, or any of the
ordinary irrational horrors of the world" yet unable (we are told
prophetically) to "withstand those more terrific, because more
spiritual terrors, which sometimes menace you from the concentrating brow of an enraged and mighty man." We know the "ig-
norant, unconscious fearlessness" of Flask—"a little waggish in
the matter of whales." We have seen Ahab throw away his pipe—
his next rejection, after his rebuke of Stubb, of his links with common humanity, which would seek only rest after toil and the
solace of creature comforts. We learn of "that certain sultanism
of his brain" which the hierarchical situation on shipboard en-
courages toward "an irresistible dictatorship." We have already
accepted the possibility (ch. 16) that out of these old Quaker whalemen might come the "globular brain," the "ponderous heart" the
"bold and nervous lofty language," of "a mighty pageant figure"
—a Job, an Oedipus, a Lear—"formed for noble tragedies." The
stage is set and the characters drawn for "the tragic dramatist"
(as Melville now openly calls himself) to present his action.

There is a preliminary lull, but full of portent, in the brief
"Mast-head" chapter, when Melville returns the story to Ishmael's
consciousness (as, occasionally, he does throughout the action)
to show the youthful novitiate's view from the crow's nest, how it
induces a mystic, Platonic reverie, providing a kind of "asylum
[in the whaling industry] for many romantic, melancholy, and
absent-minded young men, disgusted with the carking care of
earth, and seeking sentiment in tar and blubber." Here, to the
young dreamer at the masthead, the Many merge into One; the
watcher, "lulled into such an opium-like listlessness of vacant,
unconscious reverie," ceases to watch; the waves blend with his
thoughts and the sea with his soul: "he loses his identity." For a
moment we hear Ishmael talking: "For one, I used to lounge up
the rigging very leisurely, resting in the top to have a chat with
Queequeg, or any one else off duty whom I might find there...."
But it is Melville's voice that dispels this Emersonian dream, the
tragic dramatist who prepares for the full revelation. "But while
this sleep, this dream is on ye [Melville so addresses the young
dreamers], move your foot or hand an inch; slip your hold at all;
and your identity comes back in horror. Over Descartian vortices
you hover. And perhaps, at mid-day, in the fairest weather, with
one half-throttled shriek you drop through that transparent air

into the summer sea, no more to rise for ever. Heed it well, ye Pantheists!"

Ishmael was never in greater danger than on his seemingly secure and sunny perch. Here, says the tragic dramatist, was no true wisdom and therefore (in the literal sense) no true poise. Ishmael must return to the common deck and the rigors of whaling. He must know it at its worst as at its best. He must "look in the face of fire." Only then does he learn (in "The Try-Works") that "that mortal man who hath more of joy than sorrow in him, that mortal man cannot be true—not true, or undeveloped." Down from the masthead, on Ahab's own quarter-deck, a major event in Ishmael's development is about to take place.

In the Quarter-Deck scene, when with his demonic eloquence Ahab enticed the crew into his terrifying enterprise, Ishmael was confronted for the first time with a "hero" in action. Ishmael's presence as the percipient narrator is not felt during the scene; we have only his belated comment afterward. In Melville's dramatic presentation Starbuck is given the only role as antagonist to Ahab; but against the "general hurricane" of Ahab's fury, his protest in the name of common sense and respect for God's creatures could not stand. The full drama starts with this thrust of Ahab's against his destiny, against "the unknown but still reasoning thing" (as he sees it) that has worked his woe; and to this heroic fury—terrifying yet somehow appealing—Ishmael could not be a passive witness only. In the turbulent scene, all thought of comic detachment, of being sociable with horror, was for the moment overwhelmed. "I, Ishmael, was one of that crew; my shouts had gone up with the rest; my oath had been welded with theirs; and stronger I shouted, and more did I hammer and clinch my oath, because of the dread in my soul. A wild, mystical, sympathetical feeling was in me; Ahab's quenchless feud seemed mine." All of his old, reassuring categories are burst asunder in this first experience of "the dread in the soul."

But, as the voyage progressed, this dread had its abatements for Ishmael—signalizing, perhaps, how sturdy are the "admirable evasions" of average man, loath to admit his failure to domesticate the universe. Ishmael is normal, unpossessed humanity. There are moments of calm when he detaches himself from Ahab's quenchless feud and returns to his philosophizings. They are still cheerful, even if they have a new somber note, as when making mats with Queequeg, he speculates about "chance, free will, necessity," finds them "no wise incompatible—all interweavingly working together." But chance, he concludes darkly, can rule either one, and has "the last featuring blow at events." Later (ch. 49), speculating on "this strange mixed affair we call life," he slips into a sort of "desperado philosophy." In such a mood, he regards the universe as a "vast practical joke," perhaps on himself, but "with nothing to dispirit a man and nothing to dispute." He simply makes his will. "Now then, thought I, unconsciously rolling up the sleeves of my frock, here goes for a cool, collected dive at death and destruction, and the devil fetch the hindmost." Thus, argues the wise youth, if we cannot be merry, we can at least know the universe for the risky thing it is and be prepared for whatever comes. This is not Ahab's feud; it is a stoic rather than a tragic phase. It is as far, except for one other episode, as Ishmael ever gets.

If, as in *The Scarlet Letter,* there is something archetypal of all tragedy in this steady uncovering, layer by layer, of the hard meaning of existence, it is not through Ishmael's consciousness that Melville uncovers it all. Ishmael recedes as Ahab occupies the foreground. The frankly dramatic episodes (for example, The Quarter-Deck, the nine gams, The Forge, The Carpenter, the chases), like much of the whaling lore, are not controlled by Ishmael as narrator (as, for instance, the narrator Marlow controls some of Conrad's stories), nor do they reveal to us any sustained or intense spiritual struggle. A few times only, as Melville develops the "linked analogies" between whaling and human existence, is Ishmael's voice heard unmistakably. The "Monkey-Rope" episode reminds him of the precarious interdependence of human beings, how one man may innocently perish through another's error— Queequeg's, in this instance—and for a moment we hear the young tyro philosophizing again. Squeezing "case" with Queequeg puts him in mind of the friendly pressure of the hands that should bind all men together in "the very milk and sperm of kindness." But is it Ishmael's voice (or Melville's) which thanks God (in "The Fountain") that "through all the thick mists of the dim doubts in my mind, divine intuitions now and then shoot, enkindling my fog with a heavenly ray"? or, in "The Grand Armada," likens the state of his soul, "amid the tornadoed Atlantic of my being," to the calm center in the midst of the vast encircling herd of whales: "But even so...do I myself still forever centrally disport in mute calm; and while ponderous planets of unwaning woe revolve round me, deep down and deep inland there I still bathe me in eternal mildness of joy"? Who dichotomizes all men and nations, nay the great globe itself, according to the categories of Fast-Fish and Loose-Fish? All this may be a measure of Ishmael's deepening stoicism or growing philosphic poise; but actually about this time he ceases to be a fictional narrator with an autonomous spiritual development, and merges into Melville the omniscient novelist, commenting and discoursing without regard for Ishmael's fictional status or his personal point of view, and taking us within the personalities of other characters, especially Ahab and Starbuck, where Ishmael as observer could not penetrate.

Only once more before the very end do we see through Ishmael's eyes. In "The Try-Works" he knows for an awful instant what it actually feels like to be "given up" to fire. As helmsman, staring at night into the flaming try-works, he sees in the "tartarean shapes of the harpooneers," as they pitch and pole the hissing masses of blubber, "the material counterpart of [their] monomaniac commander's soul." He sees the "redness, the madness, the ghastliness," and he sees nothing else. He slips into an hypnotic drowsiness; his hold on the helm loosens, and he comes suddenly to consciousness to find himself facing dead astern. Only barely does he save the ship from being brought by the lee and possibly capsizing. He sees in his temporary distraction a sign of Ahab's moral inversion — Ahab who had looked too long on fire. Ishmael, having learned the "wisdom that is woe," now learns the "woe that is madness"; and he learns it this time on his own pulses. He learns that he is not the "Catskill eagle," nor is Ahab, who can dive down into the "blackest gorges" and rise again into the sun. "Give not thyself up, then, to fire [says Melville-Ishmael] lest it invert thee, deaden thee; as for the time it did me."

This is the last of Ishmael's intimate moral revelations. Here, except for the occasional reflections on the likeness of whaling to human life and except for the Epilogue, where he recounts only in the barest fashion the circumstances of his lone survival, we leave him. With "The Try-Works" his main function in the novel is done. He has cast off his green and dreamy youth and brought us to the edge of the vortex. The drama is now Ahab's (with Starbuck the main but ineffectual human antagonist) and Moby Dick's. The necessary probability has been established for Ahab's final plunge into the vortex itself, carrying all but Ishmael to destruction. And not since Job, as Melville's epigraph reminds us, has the destruction been so complete: "And I only am escaped alone to tell thee." All is gone, the whole "Anacharsis Clootz deputation" for the human race so devilishly misled by Ahab. The sea rolls on undisturbed as it rolled five thousand years ago. No angels sing the hero to his rest; no kingdom remains to be restored to order; only one lad just out of his novitiate lives to tell the story. Even the "bird of heaven," pinned to the mast by Tashtego's hammer, "his whole captive form folded in the flag of Ahab," goes down with the ship, which "like Satan, would not sink to hell till she had dragged a living part of heaven along with her...."

Such an ending forces to the limit any definition of tragedy comprehending positive values. We look in vain for precedents, certainly among the "Christian" heroes. Dr. Faustus had defied God and ended in hell. But he had defied God not out of hate but out of boredom or curiosity or restlessness, and in the end he had a vision of God's grace and foregiveness none the less real because he could not (or thought he could not) share in them. Lear railed at the universe but sought instruction even in his madness and learned reconciliation and love in unexpected ways. Hester lived out the dark ambiguities of her existence, with no satisfying resolution either way, but grew toward acceptance and humility rather than hate and denial. Ahab hated and denied. The universe had wronged him; he adjudged it evil and defied it. In this phase, he is a demonic, not a tragic, hero; less a Faustus or Lear or Prometheus than (as Richard Chase describes him)[3] a false Prometheus, with destruction not salvation in his heart. Ahab's is no "puritan drama of the soul," a constant tension between the vision of innocence and the accepted guilt. He rejects guilt, both when he puts himself beyond good and evil as lord and master over all the souls on the *Pequod* ("Talk not to me of blasphemy, man; I'd strike the sun if it insulted me....Who's over me?") and in his final conception of "this whole act [as] immutably decreed":

[3]Chase's treatment of Ahab ("An Approach to Melville," *Partisan Review,* May-June 1947) is surely true of one phase of his character. Ahab, says Chase, undergoes "transfiguration, not into the image of Prometheus, but into the image of the Beast-Machine.... Caught in the final violence of the whale hunt. Ahab is transfigured into the 'impersonal,' into the mechanical monster with blood on his brain" (p. 290). But this does not seem to me definitive of our total image of Ahab or even of the Ahab of the whale hunt.

"I am the Fates' lieutenant." In the first pose, Ahab is more than man—and more than tragic man; he is a self-appointed God. In the latter, he is less than man, a mere agent of destiny. To the extent that the book glorifies Ahab in these two poses and passes no further judgment on him, Melville was right in telling Hawthorne that in *Moby-Dick* he had written "a wicked book." To this extent also, it is no tragedy.

But the indictment fails to do justice to Ahab and to that in the book which is not Ahab. Ahab is an emblem of no absolute order, and the book is not a "hideous allegory" of the triumph of Evil over Good. Like the tragedies which it recalls, it is more an exploration of mysteries than a rejection of mysteries in a sweeping nihilistic gesture. Much has been made of the book as a document in Melville's personal "quarrel with God,"[4] and his rebellious accents ring (or so it would seem) unmistakably in passage after passage. But so do Melville's accents sound in Ahab's melting moods, of which there are many, and in Ahab's passages of introspection and self-doubt, as in his confession to Starbuck: "... and then, the madness, the frenzy, the boiling blood and the smoking brow, with which, for a thousand lowerings old Ahab had furiously, foamingly chased his prey—more a demon than a man—aye, aye! what a forty years' fool—fool—old fool, has old Ahab been!" Ahab "has his humanities," as Captain Peleg announced to the novitiate Ishmael at the signing on. He understands and admits (as no demonic and few romantic heroes do) his own ruthlessness —toward Pip ("Thou touchest my inmost centre, boy"), toward Starbuck, toward the captain of the *Rachel* who would engage his help in searching for the lost child. He drops his one salt tear into the great Pacific. But more than this, his feud, like Job's and Prometheus' and Lear's, is not entirely his own. He is no Byronic hero kicking himself loose from the moral universe in ironic bitterness. He took upon himself what he conceived to be the burden of humanity. He faced the darkness as he saw it. Starbuck reconciled it with his traditional beliefs; Stubb and Flask laughed it off; Ishmael saw it and adopted his "desperado philosophy."

[4]This is the theme (though disputed) of Lawrance Thompson's *Melville's Quarrel with God,* Princeton, 1952. Merrell Davis comments truly, I think, in his review of the book in *Review of English Studies,* July 1954: "In *Moby-Dick,* dealing with the problem of evil, Melville naturally uses the theological categories—and there is, of course, irony at the expense of Presbyterian orthodoxy —but, finally, Ahab is moving in the true tragic zone which is neither Christian nor Atheist...." (p. 327).

Only Ahab felt what "some deep men feel": "that intangible malignity which has been from the beginning"—whatever it is in
nature that makes these hard hearts, whatever oppresses, be-
wilders, and bears man down. Like Job and Lear, he saw his own
misfortunes as a sign of the common lot; and like them he struck
back. "He piled upon the whale's white hump the sum of all the
general rage and hate felt by his whole race from Adam down;
and then, as if his chest had been a mortar, he burst his hot heart's
shell upon it."

Should he or should he not have done what he did? Should he
or should he not have followed his "fatal pride," as Melville calls
it, to the end? If the book is to be read as saying that he *should,*
then it is a "wicked" book, justifying monomania, sultanism,
blasphemy, and the all-but-total destruction they wrought. But
the book neither justifies nor condemns Ahab. Tragedy is witness
to the moral ambiguity of every action, and Melville is true to
the witness of *Job, Dr. Faustus,* and *Lear* in conceiving of Ahab's
action in just this light. Melville keeps the precarious balance in
many ways—not only through Ismael's comments and experience
and Ahab's brooding awareness of the ethics of his action, which
comes to the surface in some of his calmer soliloquies and in his
gentler replies to Starbuck, but in the perspective that Starbuck
and the visiting captains in the gams give to Ahab's purpose; in
the constant reminder, through imagery and (later) direct comment, of the beauty, the goodness, the truth that make (with the
vision of evil) the dual vision of tragedy. Indeed, the "monomaniac"
Ahab's own statements of this duality are among the most poig-
nant: "I am dammed in the midst of Paradise." "There is that in
thee, poor lad, which I feel too curing to my malady." "So far
gone am I in the dark side of earth, that its other side, the theoretic
bright one, seems but uncertain twilight to me."

But having gone thus far in the uncertain twilight, he does not
turn back. If it grows ever darker, we are not left in total darkness. He is aware to the end of "the lovely leewardings" that he
views on his last look from the masthead. Starbuck weeps as he
clasps his hand for the last time. "Oh, my captain, my captain!—
noble heart. ..." In the end, Ahab goes down "death-glorious" like
his ship, "ungodly" yet "god-like," demonic in his own hate and
vengeance, yet noble in his sense of the community of all unjust
suffering. The book does not pronounce him good or evil any
more than *The Scarlet Letter* calls Hester Prynne good or evil.

But by carrying him through his fatal action in all its tensions, paradoxes, and ambiguities, the book, like a true tragedy, goes deeply into the mysteries of all moral judgments. All categories are put to the sharpest test, not only Ishmael's, Starbuck's, Stubb's, and Flask's but Ahab's own. We see the nature of each, how far toward good-and-evil each can go. The book leaves us, again true to its tradition, somewhere between pity and terror, faith and doubt, heaven and hell; it leaves us in what Ishmael-Melville calls (in "The Gilder") "manhood's pondering repose of If." But we have seen the conditions of pity and terror, good and evil, heaven and hell, more clearly. "Doubts of all things earthly, and intuitions of some things heavenly; this combination makes neither believer nor infidel, but makes a man who regards them both with equal eye."

Ahab himself never achieved such repose or looked on life so steadily, or if he did it was only momentarily. One other momentary insight comes to him in the frenzy of his final battle with the whale, and in a way it is his climactic insight. The perennial sense of injustice, the cry of Prometheus and Job as of Lear and Hamlet, was also Ahab's. Why do the innocent suffer? "O cursed spite/ That ever I was born to set it right." This was the "inscrutable thing" that Ahab hated. Ahab never penetrated the mystery nor came to as full an understanding of the meaning in suffering as did Job or Lear. But in the moment of final conflict he senses a new dimension in his suffering, a relatedness to something other than the sheer malice of the universe, the whiteness of the whale.

As Ahab in his whaleboat watches the *Pequod* founder under the attack of the whale, he realizes that all is lost. He faces his "lonely death on lonely life," denied even "the last fond pride of meanest shipwrecked captains," the privilege of going down with his ship. But here, at the nadir of his fortunes, he sees that in his greatest suffering lies his greatest glory. He dies spitting hate at the whale, but he does not die cynically or in bitterness. The whale conquers—but is "unconquering." The "god-bullied hull" goes down "death-glorious." What Ahab feels is not joy, or serenity, or goodness at the heart of things. But with his sense of elation, even triumph, at having persevered to the end, there is also a note of reconciliation: "Oh, now I feel my topmost greatness lies in my topmost grief." This is not reconciliation with the whale, or with the malice in the universe, but it is a reconciliation of Ahab with Ahab. Whatever justice, order, or equivalence there is, he has found not in the universe but in himself.[5] He is neither "sultan" now nor "old fool." In finally coming to terms with existence (though too late), he is tragic man; to the extent that he transcends it, finds "greatness" in suffering, he is tragic hero.

Melville did not dramatize further this final phase of Ahab's course, and therein lies the peculiarly shocking nature of the book. It is as if we left Job at the end of one of his diatribes or Oedipus at his self-blinding or Lear as he curses his daughters and plunges into the storm. Even with this final insight of Ahab's, the ending seems too dire for tragedy. It seems to deny the future; when the *Pequod* sinks, all seems lost; and there is no further comment, no fifth-act compensations to let in a little hope. The only comment is the action itself, the total action from beginning to end, all the good and the evil it uncovers. There is one survivor of the action: the tragic artist to tell about it from beginning to end. In the chapter called "Brit," Melville writes: "…man has lost that sense of the full awfulness of the sea which aboriginally belongs to it"; and the sea, he reminds us shortly, covers "two thirds of the fair world." *Moby-Dick* presents this awfulness relentlessly, even wickedly, as Melville hinted to Hawthorne. It is a cruel reminder of the original terror. If the world it presents is the starkest kind of answer to the Emersonian dream, it is not a world for despair or rejection — as long as there is even one who escapes to tell its full story.

[5] Henry Alonzo Myers, in *Tragedy: A View of Life* (Ithaca, Cornell University Press, 1956), ch. 3, "The Tragic Meaning of *Moby-Dick,*" calls this "Ahab's great discovery and the key to the tragic meaning of *Moby-Dick*" (p. 72). He goes on: "The end of Ahab is not unrelieved defeat, but victory in defeat; and the main point of *Moby-Dick* is that any great human action will show that the heavens and the deeps, eternal symbols of man's triumphs and disasters, are merely the limits of his experience, related to each other through that experience and dependent upon each other and upon him for their meaning" (p. 73). Ahab, "neither saint nor sinner" but with a "grand passion to do and to know," discovered in the end that "the only compensations for his fate are to be found in himself, in the nature that is capable of an exaltation exactly equal to his grief…. Ahab's victory equals his defeat, his joy equals his sorrow" (pp. 74-75). Although there is much in this, and in this fine essay, which seems to me true, I find it difficult to accommodate Myers' idea of exact equivalence into what I think this tragedy (and tragedy in general) says. Does Ahab's final joy equal his sorrow? Like Job, Ahab never got an answer to his question. He never "penetrated the mask." The metaphor of "equivalence" suggests, I think, too neat and precise an equation. The metaphor of precarious and imperfect balance, to which I have had occasional recourse in this study, is none too satisfactory; but it suggests the constant opposition of forces, the unremitting tension, which I find true of tragedy.

Ahab and His Fool

by Charles Olson

Life has its way, even with Ahab. Melville had drawn upon another myth besides Shakespeare's to create his dark Ahab, that of both Marlowe and Goethe: the Faust legend. But he alters it. After the revolutions of the 18th-19th century the archetype Faust has never been the same. In Melville's alteration the workings of Lear and the Fool can also be discerned.

The change comes in the relation of Ahab to Pip. Ahab does not die in the tempestuous agony of Faustus pointing to Christ's blood and crying for His mercy. He dies with an acceptance of his damnation. Before his final battle with the White Whale Ahab has resigned himself to his fate.

His solipsism is most violent and his hate most engendered the night of THE CANDLES when he raises the burning harpoon over his crew. It is a night of storm. The setting is *Lear*-like. Ahab, unlike Lear, does not in this night of storm discover his love for his fellow wretches. On the contrary, this night Ahab uncovers his whole hate. He commits the greater blasphemy than defiance of sun and lightning. He turns the harpoon, forged and baptized for the inhuman Whale alone, upon his own human companions, the crew, and brandishes his hate over them. The morning after the storm Ahab is most subtly dedicated to his malignant purpose when he gives the lightning-twisted binnacle a new needle. Melville marks this pitch of his ego:

> In his fiery eyes of scorn and triumph, you then saw Ahab in all his fatal pride.

In a very few hours the change in Ahab sets in and Pip—the shadow of Pip—is the agent of the change. Like a reminder of Ahab's soul he calls to Ahab and Ahab, advancing to help, cries

to the sailor who has seized Pip: "Hands off that holiness!" It is
a crucial act: for the first time Ahab has offered to help another
human being. And at that very moment Ahab speaks Lear's phrases:

> Thou touchest my inmost centre, boy; thou art tied to me by cords
> woven of my heart-strings. Come, let's down.

Though Ahab continues to curse the gods for their "inhumanities,"
his tone, from this moment, is richer, quieter, less angry and
strident. He even questions his former blasphemies, for a bot-
tomed sadness grows in him as Pip lives in the cabin with him.
There occurs a return of something Peleg had insisted that Ahab
possessed on the day Ishmael signed for the fatal voyage. Peleg
then refuted Ishmael's fears of his captain's wicked name—that
dogs had licked his blood. He revealed that Ahab had a wife and
child, and concluded:

> hold ye then there can be any utter, hopeless harm in Ahab? No,
> no, my lad; stricken, blasted, if he be, Ahab has his humanities!

These humanities had been set aside in Ahab's hate for the White
Whale. One incident: Ahab never thought, as he paced the deck
at night in fever of anger, how his whalebone stump rapping the
boards waked his crew and officers. The aroused Stubb confronts Ahab. Ahab orders him like a dog to kennel. For Stubb
cannot, like Pip, affect Ahab. When it is over Stubb's only impulse
is to go down on his knees and pray for the hot old man who he
feels has so horribly amputated himself from human feelings.

Pip continues to be, mysteriously, the agent of this bloom once
it has started. Says Ahab: "I do suck most wondrous philosophies
from thee!" He even goes so far as to ask God to bless Pip and
save him. BUT before he asks that, he threatens to murder Pip,
Pip so weakens his revengeful purpose.

Though Pip recedes in the last chapters, the suppleness he has
brought out of old Ahab continues to grow. Pip is left in the hold
as though Ahab would down his soul once more, but above decks
Ahab is no longer the proud Lucifer. He asks God to bless the
captain of the *Rachel*, the last ship they meet before closing with
Moby Dick, the vessel which later picks Ishmael up after the
tragedy. The difference in his speech is commented on: "a voice
that prolongingly moulded every word." And it is noticed that
when, toward the last days, Ahab prepares a basket lookout for
himself to be hoisted up the mast to sight Moby Dick, he trusts

his "life-line" to Starbuck's hands. This running sap of his humanities give out its last shoots in THE SYMPHONY chapter: observe that Ahab asks God to destroy what has been from the first his boast—"God! God! God! stave my brain!" He has turned to Starbuck and talked about his wife and child! And though this apple, his last, and cindered, drops to the soil, his revenge is now less pursued than resigned to. His thoughts are beyond the whale, upon easeful death.

In the three days' chase he is a tense, mastered, almost grim man. He sets himself outside humanity still, but he is no longer arrogant, only lonely: "Cold, cold…" After the close of the second day, when Fedallah cannot be found, he withers. His last vindictive shout is to rally his angers which have been hurled and lost like Fedallah and the harpoon of lightning and blood. He turns to Fate, the handspike in his windlass: "The whole act's immutably decreed." That night he does not face the whale as was his custom. He turns his "heliotrope glance" back to the east, waiting the sun of the fatal third day like death. It is Macbeth in his soliloquy of tomorrow, before Macduff will meet and match him. On the third day the unbodied winds engage his attention for the first time in the voyage. Even after the White Whale is sighted Ahab lingers, looks over the sea, considers his ship, says goodbye to his masthead. He admits to Starbuck he foreknows his death: the prophecies are fulfilled. In his last speech he moans only that his ship perishes without him:

> Oh, lonely death on lonely life! Oh, now I feel my topmost greatness lies in my topmost grief.

He rushes to the White Whale with his old curse dead on his lips.

The last words spoken to him from the ship had been Pip's: "Oh master, my master, come back!"

What Pip wrought in Ahab throws over the end of *Moby-Dick* a veil of grief, relaxes the tensions of its hate, and permits a sympathy for the stricken man that Ahab's insistent diabolism up to the storm would not have evoked. The end of this fire-forked tragedy is enriched by a pity in the very jaws of terror.

The lovely association of Ahab and Pip is like the relations of Lear to both the Fool and Edgar. What the King learns of their suffering through companionship with them in storm helps him to shed his pride. His hedging and self-deluding authority gone,

Lear sees wisdom in their profound unreason. He becomes capable of learning from his Fool just as Captain Ahab does from his cabin-boy.

In *Lear* Shakespeare has taken the conventional "crazy-witty" and brought him to an integral place in much more than the plot. He is at center to the poetic and dramatic conception of the play. Melville grasped the development.

Someone may object that Pip is mad, not foolish. In Shakespeare the gradations subtly work into one another. In *Moby-Dick* Pip is both the jester and the idiot. Before he is frightened out of his wits he and his tambourine are cap and bells to the crew. His soliloquy upon their midnight revelry has the sharp, bitter wisdom of the Elizabethan fool. And his talk after his "drowning" is parallel not only to the Fool and Edgar but to Lear himself.

A remark in *Moby-Dick* throws a sharp light over what has just been said and over what remains to be said. Melville comments on Pip:

> all thy strange mummeries not unmeaningly blended with the black tragedy of the melancholy ship, and mocked it.

For Pip by his madness had seen God.

Moby-Dick: Jonah's Whale or Job's?

by Daniel Hoffman

I

Myth as Metaphor

"There are some enterprises in which a careful disorderliness is the true method," Melville writes in *Moby-Dick*. His
curious phrase suggests the delicate balance he had to maintain
between the multitudinous metaphors that poured forth from his
imagination and the prefiguration which had to be applied to
their arrangement. Melville, as Constance Rourke suggested,
"used the familiar method of the legend-maker, drawing an ac-
cumulation of whaling lore from many sources, much of it from
New England, some of it hearsay, some from books, including
stories of the adventures of other ships encountered at sea, or
further tales suggested by episodes within the main sequence of
his story." Among those who have observed the fact, Matthiessen
has said it best: "In his effort to endow the whaling industry with
a mythology befitting a fundamental activity of man in his struggle
to subdue nature, [Melville] came into possession of the primitive energies latent in words."[1] Not only does Melville make his
own metaphors and endow them with the universal qualities of
myths, but he also draws deeply on the mythic formulations of
experience already available to him. Although there are dim
prefigurations in his earlier romances of what he was to do in
Moby-Dick, Melville found his mature purpose and the means of

Moby-Dick: Jonah's Whale or Job's?", by Daniel Hoffman. From *Form and
Fable in American Fiction* by Daniel Hoffman (New York: Oxford University
Press, 1961), pp. 233-36, 256-62, 269-78. Copyright © 1961 by Daniel G. Hoffman.
Reprinted by permission of the author. The version printed here originally
appeared in *The Sewanee Review,* 69 (Spring 1961), 205-24, and differs in minor
respects from the Oxford University Press edition.

[1]Constance Rourke, *American Humor* (New York, 1931), p. 194; F. O. Matthiessen, *American Renaissance* (New York, 1941), p. 423.

fulfilling it in the process of writing his greatest book. His mythical themes seem to leap fully-formed from his mind. We may observe that he draws together the mythical patterns of several
cultures and of several levels within his own culture: the primitive ritual, the Greek myth, the Biblical legend, the folklore of
supernatural dread and wonder (common to both the Old World
and the New), and the specifically American folk traditions of
comic glorification, of Yankee and frontier character. And in the
"careful disorderliness" which is "the true method" of *Moby-
Dick* these themes from myth, folklore, and ritual are ranged in
a series of dialectical contrasts which dramatize and unify the
several controlling tensions of the work.

Among these tensions the chief are those between the two
examples of the hero. The contrary commitments of Ahab and
Ishmael are dramatized in large part by their respective alle-
giances to certain heroes of Old World myth and of New World
folklore. The narrative of the hunt embodies the seminal myth
of a divinely-endowed hero who in hand-to-hand combat rids
his people of the evil monster that was their scourge. Ahab appears to belong in the company in which Ishmael jocularly en-
rolls himself: among Perseus, Theseus, and Saint George. (Ishmael
maintains that Cetus, the Medusa and the dragon, being sea-
creatures, were necessarily whales.) But Ahab in fact differs from
these prototypical figures in being a false culture-hero, pursuing
a private grievance (rather than a divine behest) at the expense of
the mankind in his crew. He is more properly a Faust who has
sold his soul to the devil (who is aboard as Fedallah the fire-
worshipper). A Faust who commands and enchants his followers
becomes, as Ahab does, a Satan, a sorcerer, an Anti-Christ.

The lowly sailor, contrarily, is humanely adaptable and receptive to experience. Ishmael's style, the doubly comic and fearful
cast of his imagination, and his metamorphic career all relate
him to the qualities of the American folk character. His own in-
volvement in the adventure he records takes the unsought but
intrinsic form of initiation and rebirth. Indeed, for all aboard
the *Pequod* the voyage is one of search and discovery, the search
for the ultimate truth of experience. But each seeker can make
only those discoveries his own character has preordained as
possible for him. Ishmael's initiation is revealed through the
pattern of the hunt whose object becomes known only when the
crew is welded to their mad commander's purpose by the magical

rites which Ahab as Anti-Christ performs on the quarter-deck. Then "Ahab's crazy quest seemed mine." But Ishmael discovers a deeper magic, a more potent source of supernatural energy, and dissolves this specious bond of Ahab's with a counter-ritual of his own. The brotherhood of violence to which Ahab bound him proves to be the self-destructive moral nihilism of selfhood uncontrolled. Freed by his discovery, in "A Squeeze of the Hand," of the organic unity of man with fellow-man, Ishmael wins his right to be the "sole survivor" of the final catastrophe. Cast up by the sea, he is saved by the coffin prepared for his boon companion Queequeg the cannibal, to whom the bonds of human love had bound him closest.

Opposed to the legend of the mighty hero are other mythical patterns in *Moby-Dick* which dramatize the contraries to Ahab's aggression against the inscrutable forces in the universe. The Hunter may be not only an aggressor but a Seeker, a seeker after truth. Opposed to Ahab's power and defiance is love. But love, to be an effective counter-principle, must find its proper object; should love turn inward, rather than embrace the "Not-Me," it becomes its own opposite, the wish for death. One of the manifestations of love in *Moby-Dick* occurs in versions of the myth of Narcissus, who, falling in love with his own image, destroyed himself. In the Narcissus myth, which Melville invokes in the very first chapter (and often again), the hunter becomes both a seeker and a solipsist. Yet it is the power of love alone, an outward-reaching love, that can overcome the wished-for death, as Ishmael but not Ahab learns.

When the hunt is for a whale who seems to embody divine power, when the Hunters and Seekers are also Rebels against divinity or candidates for repentance and redemption, it is inevitable that the Biblical legend of Jonah govern much of the metaphor and the action. In fact Melville introduces this myth into the narrative early too, taking from the Book of Jonah the text for Father Mapple's sermon. That Christian sermon states the ethical desiderata against which the fates of Ahab, Ishmael, and the rest are subsequently measured. Part of their fate is to relive aspects of Jonah's rebellion against God's Word, his incarceration in the whale, his being cast forth, and his redemption. Only Ishmael can reenact the entire myth; for the others, to each is given his own portion of Jonah's suffering, wisdom, and glory.

These then are the executive metaphors from mythology and

folklore which give this prodigious book much of its inner co-
herence. The oppositions within the romance of the claims of
aggression and passivity, of hostility and acceptance, of defiance
and of submission to the "Divine Inert," are consistently proposed and elaborated by these masterful myth-symbols. The
interstices of the action are braced by the enactment of rituals —
among the most important are the "marriage" of Ishmael and
Queequeg, the cannibal's worship of his idol, Father Mapple's
sermon and the cook's, Ahab's black mass on the quarter-deck,
Ishmael's cleansing of his soul in the spermaceti, and the final
annihilating catastrophe. The work is yet almost everywhere
saved from becoming what Melville shunned as "a hideous and
intolerable allegory" by his insistence upon tangible fact: the
reality of an actual ship and live whales, of a particular captain
and his crew, and the documentation which makes *Moby-Dick* a
guide to all of the operations of the whaling industry.

II
A Voyage to Nineveh

In the world of *Moby-Dick* nothing exists without its opposite
and no vision which fails to encompass both poles of every contrast can embrace the truth. The qualities Melville dramatized
through the Narcissus myth are necessarily in tension with their
opposites, and those qualities inhere in another legendary nexus
of images: the Jonah story. This theme is early introduced by
Father Mapple's sermon in chapter 9. When Narcissus as Seeker
leaned toward "the mild image in the fountain," Jonah as Rebel
tries to flee by water from the command of God. Where Narcissus
proves a solipsist, the rebel Jonah at last acknowledges the God
beyond himself. In consequence Jonah is not, like Narcissus, a
suicide, but is reborn, literally resurrected from his death inside
the whale. These experiences of Jonah's prove to be prototypes
of several adventures suffered not only by Ishmael and Ahab but
also by the harpooners Tashtego and Queequeg and by the de-
mented cabin-boy Pip.

It is essential that we recognize these not only as Biblical parallels
but also as the enactments of the ritual significance of the Jonah
story itself. That story, as William Simpson demonstrated in *The*

Jonah Legend (London, 1899), is in fact the account of an initiation ceremony in which the candidate for admission to divine knowledge at first ceremonially rebels against submission to the divine behest, the "Not-Me"; then undergoes a symbolic mock-death in the whale's belly (actually, a vault below the floor of the temple);[2] and emerges reborn into the cult or priesthood.

Melville, writing half a century before Simpson, yet had access to the very evidence the later theologian would, with the help of Frazer's anthropology, systematize into his ritual interpretation. Drawing on both Pierre Bayle's *Historical and Critical Dictionary* and John Kitto's recently issued *Cyclopedia of Biblical Literature,* Melville found the very rationalistic hypotheses which the later theologian would use to support his contention that the Biblical Jonah legend was in fact a late variant of an ancient initiation ritual. These two sources of Melville's take opposite views of the same evidence (it is probable that Kitto drew on Bayle, disputing the Frenchman's skepticism, for his articles on "Jonah" and "Whale"). Melville mined whole paragraphs from both, sportively adopting the very rationalizations of the legend which the Frenchman proposed and which the pious encyclopedist had been at pains to discredit.

Melville, however, can make the descent into the whale just as literal as it seems in the Book of Jonah, as he does when Tashtego falls into the severed head of a dead sperm. Or he can describe the *Pequod* in similes suggesting the ship itself as a whale: "A cannibal of a craft"—as though she would swallow her crew—"tricking herself forth in the chased bones of her enemies," her bulwarks "garnished like one continuous jaw, with the long sharp teeth of the sperm whale," and her tiller "carved from the long narrow jaw of her hereditary foe." The similitude is already established in Father Mapple's text: "Beneath the ship's water-line, Jonah feels the heralding presentiment of that stifling hour, when the whale shall hold him in the smallest of his bowels' wards."

The conventional Christian interpretation of Jonah proposes his "death" and resurrection after three days in the whale as a prefiguration of Christ's rising. Melville consistently presents Ahab, his Anti-Christ, in the guise of an unrepentant Jonah.

[2]In the prefatory "Etymology" Melville cites as one origin of the word *whale* the Danish *hvalt,* "arched or vaulted."

Ahab's disobedience of God's commands foredooms the voyage;[3] his aggressive will, we recognize, is in flight from truth rather than possessing it. His godless purpose provokes the elements themselves at the *Pequod's* first pursuit of a whale. As they strike the whale, the storm strikes them; the ship looms through the mist and the frightened boat's crew cast themselves into the sea. But where Jonah confessed his apostasy and the crew threw him overboard, Ahab's "confession" on the quarter-deck puts his entire crew in league with him. The Anti-Christ is at this stage an Anti-Jonah, welcoming the catastrophe his own mad pride had created. Father Mapple had warned, "Delight—top-gallant delight is to him, who acknowledges no law or lord, but the Lord his God, and is only a patriot to heaven." This delight Ahab can never know, who blindly refuses to disobey himself. But Ahab meets his end as though it were a triumph; although he dies, Moby Dick has proved to be the "outrageous strength, with an inscrutable malice sinewing it; whether agent or principal," which Ahab hates, and in death Ahab merges at last with the uncontrollable power he pressed his pulse against when the corpusants blazed above him. Even some part of Jonah's delight is his after all: "And eternal delight and deliciousness will be his, who coming to lay him down, can say with his final breath—O Father!—Known to me chiefly by Thy rod—mortal or immortal, here I die." For the Hebraic-Calvinistic God of the Nantucket sailors' Bethel *is*, in the end, patristic, unknowable power. Compounded of heretical apostasies though Ahab's woe-reaping monism may be, he is yet on his own terms triumphant in defeat, acknowledging the justice of his dreadful punishment. But Ahab's terms are those of the sterile, regressive, annihilation-seeking solipsist. Having made himself into a destructive machine, he must perish without hope of resurrection.

Ishmael's original disobedience would consist in the "damp, drizzly November in his soul," the denial of life that brought him, too, to the *Pequod's* wharf. (The sketch of the blacksmith, chapter 112, suggests that this death-wish is a universal motive.) Ishmael had said "The world's a ship on its passage out." He was in the boat that chased the first whale in the storm, and when the *Pequod* loomed out of the mist he too leapt into the sea.

[3]In his earlier assault against God's command (on the previous voyage) the whale had given him warning of God's will by *swallowing only his leg*. Ahab is maddened rather than forewarned.

"Saved" by the ship, the *Pequod* for him becomes the whale it so curiously resembles. When it sinks, he is cast forth as Jonah was spewed from the mouth of the fish.

Although Ishmael more completely than the rest enacts Jonah's initiatory ritual, he does so in the presence not of Jonah's God but of Job's. Jonah's God, as Matthew 12:40 tells us, becomes God the Merciful Father of Jesus: "For as Jonas was three days and three nights in the heart of the earth." And the next verse prophesies that "The men of Nineveh shall rise in Judgment with this generation, and shall condemn it: because they repented at the preaching of Jonas." When we compare Father Mapple's sermon to the Book of Jonah we are struck by Melville's suppression of the sequel to Jonah's deliverance from the whale; his Jonah does not propose to God vengeance against the sinners of Nineveh, nor is he chastened by the parable of the gourd, illustrating God's infinite mercy.

The fifth "Extract" is especially significant: "In that day, the Lord with his sore, and great, and strong sword, shall punish Leviathan the piercing serpent, even Leviathan that crooked serpent, and he shall slay the dragon that is in the sea." (Isa. 21:1) Here is biblical support for both Ishmael's contention that whalemen are the culture-heroes of antiquity and for Ahab's contention of his self-appointed destiny. It is of course the fatality of Ahab's hubris that he sees himself as the lordly avenger slaying the tangible shape of evil. But Ishmael, just after the quarter-deck, declares Ahab (in chapter 41) to be an "ungodly old man, chasing with curses a Job's whale round the world." After Ishmael has endured the annihilation Ahab willed, he begins his epilogue with the words of Job's messengers of destruction: "And I only am escaped alone to tell thee."

But who is "thee," and what message is Ishmael alone escaped to tell? He survives to preach to *us,* his Nineveh, as Father Mapple had said of Jonah who "did the Almighty's bidding. And what was that, shipmates? To preach the Truth to the face of Falsehood! That was it!"

Yet Ishmael's "Truth" is neither the submission of Jonah to God's will nor the still more Christian humility Father Mapple proposed as "top-gallant delight." How far Ishmael-Melville was from accepting the "Divine Inert" as his guide to this world is apparent from the contrast between Ishmael and Pip. For Pip's actions parallel Jonah's being cast away and Christ's resurrection, but at the cost of his accommodation to any life in this world. In a chapter titled "The Castaway" we learn how little Pip on his first whale chase had leapt in terror into the sea and was abandoned as Stubb pursued the whale. "The intense concentration of self in the middle of such a heartless immensity, my God! who can tell it?" When saved by the ship,

> the little negro went about the deck an idiot. . . . The sea had jeering-ly kept his finite body up, but drowned the infinite of his soul. Not drowned entirely, though. Rather carried down alive to wond-rous depths where strange shapes of the unwarped primal world glided to and fro before his passive eyes. . . . He saw God's foot upon the treadle of the loom, and spoke it; and therefore his shipmates called him mad. So man's insanity is heaven's sense.

Pip's resurrection is entirely spiritual—his very name, Pip, for Pippin, suggests Matthew 13:38, "the good seed are the children of the kingdom." Losing his earthly senses, he participates in glory. In his gibberish he plays Fool to Ahab's Lear; in his sancti-ty, Good Angel to Ahab's Faust. Unheeded, Pip yet brings the New Testament God of Mercy and Transfiguration before the mind that conceives only of the Old Testament God of Wrath, vengeance and destruction. "Hands off that holiness!" Ahab cries, acknowledging the godliness in Pip that he has inverted and denied in himself. Ishmael may have Pip's transcendent glory in mind when he says, at the end of "The Castaway," "In the sequel of the narrative it will then be seen what like abandon-ment befell myself." Pip is in glory already; Ishmael, saved like Jonah from the whale, has yet to endure his span of life with the knowledge of God won at last by all his senses from experience of that whale. And the whale, as he had said, was "a Job's whale."

Tashtego's deliverance was more literally Jonah-like, since his peril was to have fallen into the head of a whale. Where Pip is spiritually "saved," the redemption of Tashtego is emphatically physical. Queequeg leaps overboard, knife in hand, cuts his way into the now sinking head, and by dint of "agile obstetrics," rescues Tashtego "in the good old way, head-first," in "a running delivery." This is but one of Queequeg's several acknowledge-ments of the divine law of love which makes him, at life's risk, assume responsibility for his fellow-man—first a bumpkin on a New Bedford schooner, later Ishmael himself; and, in the end, Queequeg proffers the coffin prepared for his sickness as a life-preserver with 30 life-lines, for the entire crew. Tashtego's rebirth from the whale keeps the Jonah imagery afloat in mid-passage, but it is focused throughout on Ahab's rebellion and Ishmael's survival. Queequeg is the agent both of Tashtego's delivery and of Ishmael's. But the cannibal's part in Ishmael's "delivery" is not merely to provide the coffin-lifebuoy, important as that is. Queequeg's love redeems Ishmael from the fatal isolation which had led him to choose Ahab's ship for his journey away from his self. He must lose himself to find himself. His love for Queequeg makes this possible, and qualifies Ishmael, alone of Ahab's oath-bound crew, to dissever the bonds of hatred and vengeance and so qualify for survival from the annihilation that Ahab willed for all the rest.

III
God's Whale

Father Mapple's sermon early proposed the Christian ethic by which all subsequent actions are measured. How cruelly inapplicable this transcendent ethic is to the microcosm of the *Pequod* is dramatized in its seeming parody, the cook's sermon to the sharks. Stubb, the second mate, has killed a whale and must have the cook prepare him a steak for supper. Venting his vein of Mike Fink's frontier humor, the mate bullies the old Negro into preaching a sermon to the sharks swarming about the whale's carcass, "mingling their mumblings with his own mastications." The sermon is comic in the fashion of frontier dialect humor. "Your woraciousness, fellow-critters, I don't blame ye so much for: dat is natur, and can't be helped; but to gobern dat wicked nature, dat is de pint. You is sharks, sartin, but if you gobern de shark in you, why den you be angel...." "Well done, old Fleece, that's Christianity," cried Stubb.

Father Mapple's Christianity is meaningless in such a sharkish world. Only Pip, whose soul did not know the savagery necessary to the true whaler, the mortal man, can attain the selflessness of the Sermon on the Mount. The only other practicing Christian on the *Pequod* is the first mate, Starbuck. And he is described as suffering "the incompetence of mere unaided virtue or right-mindedness." Although physically no coward, the mate "cannot withstand those more terrific, because more spiritual terrors, which sometimes menace you from the concentrating brow of an enraged and mighty man." Living by his own code of Christian charity, he yet fails in what Ishmael presents to us as a higher law: active rebellion against active evil. Starbuck alone has the temporal authority, intelligence, and moral perception to over-throw Ahab's wicked tyranny and thus save all the crew. But he lacks the power to meet power with power; twice he might kill Ahab yet cannot pull the trigger, cannot let fall the rope; twice he might raise a mutiny, yet fails at the quarter deck and fails at the last chase, just as he always fails to dissuade Ahab from mad-ness. Starbuck's unfulfilled duties are made plain by the inter-polated fable of "The Town-Ho's Story" in which a subordinate's rebellion against a tyrannous mate is given divine sanction—by Moby Dick.

Nature does not accommodate or condone the failure to meet amoral force with force, what though power itself corrupt. Nature, God's own creation, is not pure, but sharkish, vulturish, cannibal-istic, horrible. And Ishmael, we have been told, knows himself a cannibal, ever ready to rebel against even his savage king. Christianity as Melville knew it was unequal to the needs his faith must fulfill. On one side it led to the repression of Eros, the worship of force, to Ahab's emasculation of humanity; on the other, to Starbuck's ineffectual passivity or to the super-human acceptance of the Divine Inert—Pip's mindless purity, which proves effeminate, passive, deathlike.

What faith Melville proposes through Ishmael's initiation is of course determined by the nature of his God. In the rituals of non-Christian worship and in the entire constellation of legends, superstitions, and beliefs about the whale we may find at last the lineaments of Deity in *Moby-Dick*.

To find his God, his father, had been Ahab's quest; his method he foretold in saying "All visible objects, man, are but as paste-board masks....If man will strike, strike through the mask!" Ahab's violence, projecting itself through the mask of appear-ances, never doubts that anything but itself lurks there: Narcissus as avenger.

But once in this book, though, Ishmael does see what lies behind the pasteboard mask. In his bedchamber at the Spouter Inn was "a papered fireboard representing a man striking a whale." Queequeg's first act on entering—before he even knows that

Ishmael is in the room — is to remove this paper screen, and, there between the sooty firedogs, *he himself put the image of his own god*. The pasteboard mask conceals nothing that man has not put there.

Queequeg's idol is a black figurine named Yojo, who later counsels the cannibal to let Ishmael choose the ship of their adventure. After they have heard Father Mapple preach together, Ishmael, by now "married" to his friend, "must turn idolator," kindle Yojo's fire, and salaam to the pagan deity. What I take all this to mean is that the source of redemptive love is, for Melville, a divinity pre-Christian[4] and pre-rational. (This is why Queequeg invokes Yojo before being aware of Ishmael's presence.) But Yojo, the pagan love-god, is not the creator of the universe. The white whale seems as close as we can come to touching that power and awful beauty.

Yet neither is Moby Dick God; he is God's whale — and Job's whale. Ahab mistook God's power for God's essence, and heaped on that white hump "the intangible malignity which has been from the beginning...all the subtle demonisms of life and thought." To Ishmael, however, the most terrifying aspect of the whale's whiteness is "a colorless all-color of atheism," the ever-present possibility of cosmic nothingness, in which "the palsied universe lies before us a leper." All of Ishmael's explorations of the attempts made in art, science, folklore and myth, to define the whale are a contradictory labyrinth of suppositions which only his own experience can verify. And that experience proves the white whale unknowable to the last. If, then, we cannot know God's greatest handiwork, how can we know the God that made him?

On this reef many an interpreter of *Moby-Dick* has foundered. It seems hard to resist Ahab's incantatory power and not agree with him, that the white whale is indeed the immanent God of this work, even though one reject Ahab's definition of His nature.

---

[4] Yojo is the same color as the whale's phallus and as that priapic idol which Queen Maachah worshipped and Asa, her son, destroyed and "burnt for an abomination at the brook of Kedron, as darkly set forth in the fifteenth chapter of the first book of Kings" (ch. 95; cf. I Ki. 15:13). Melville surely invented this obscure comparison (the Bible does not even darkly hint at the color of the Queen's idol) because at the very place where Asa burnt the phallic image, Judas betrayed Jesus (John: 18:1-5). Christianity and the sensual Eros are mutually exclusive in *Moby-Dick*.

But Moby Dick is no more the God of *Moby-Dick* than Leviathan is the God of the Book of Job. The inscrutable whale, titanic in power, lovely in motion, ubiquitous in space, immortal in time, is the ultimate demonstration and absolute convincement of all anarchic, individualistic, egotistical, human doubt that there is a God beyond the powers of man to plumb. Melville's God lies beyond even the Gospel truths. He is Job's God, not Jonah's prefiguration of Christ's rising. That is why Ishmael ends his tale with the words of the messengers of calamity.

It is hard to unmingle the knowledge of God's essence from the knowledge of His power. Ahab must grasp the chain-link to feel the living lightning against his own pulse, power participating in power. Ishmael, too, touches the will of deity by an act which the linked analogies of his metaphoric mind makes analagous to the will of godhead. This act is the weaving of the sword-mat (ch. 47). Just before the first whale was sighted, Ishmael and Queequeg together wove a mat to protect their boat. Ishmael's own hand was the shuttle; Queequeg drove a wooden "sword" between the threads to straighten the woof. Ishmael elaborates this scene in the manner of a Puritan preacher, making an extended conceit from homely images of common labor; as he speaks here of the most urgent philosophic problem of the book, a rather long quotation must be introduced:

> ...it seemed as if this were the Loom of Time, and I myself were a shuttle mechanically weaving and weaving away at the Fates. There lay the fixed threads of the warp subject to but one single, ever returning, unchanging vibration, and that vibration merely enough to admit of the crosswise interblending of other threads with its own. This warp seemed necessity; and here, thought I, with my own hand I ply my own shuttle and weave my own destiny into these unalterable threads. Meanwhile, Queequeg's impulsive, indifferent sword, sometimes hitting the wood slantingly, or crookedly, or strongly, or weakly, as the case might be; and by this difference in the concluding blow producing a corresponding contrast in the final aspect of the completed fabric; this savage's sword, thought I, which thus finally shapes and fashions both warp and woof; this easy, indifferent sword must be chance—aye, chance, free will, and necessity—no wise incompatible—all inter-weavingly working together. The straight warp of necessity, not to be swerved from its ultimate course—its very alternating vibration, indeed, only tending to that; free will still free to ply her shuttle between

given threads; and chance, though restrained in its play within the right lines of necessity, and sidewise in its motions directed by free will, though thus prescribed to by both, chance by turns rules either, and has the last featuring blow at events.

At the savage lookout's first cry "There she blows!" "the ball of free will dropped from my hand."

Ishmael's quest from the beginning is to seek out and read the pattern of the loom. The opening chapter is called "Loomings"; the pun on "weavings" and the nautical term for something hidden below the horizon coming into view is but the first hint of Ishmael's comedic acceptance of what Father Mapple's hymn calls the "terrible" and the "joyful" in his earthly life. The weaving image (though somewhat contrived in the sword-mat passage) itself represents both the creative and dynamic elements in Ishmael's view of the cosmos. The loom is still a-weaving, the pattern ever emergent, never complete. Such a view is directly antithetical to Ahab's rigid and mechanical conception of his destiny: "This whole act's immutably decreed....I am the Fates' lieutenant." Ishmael's loom metaphor knits together the clusters of images involving lines, ropes, and shrouds, realistically present on a sailing-ship but imaginatively made to ply the loom of Fate on which each thread adds its color and direction to the grand design. "What depths of the soul Jonah's deep sealine sound!" preached Father Mapple; "Shipmates, it is a two-stranded lesson." The strands of life and of death appear in later lines, especially "the magical, sometimes horrible whaleline." "All men live enveloped in whale-lines. All men are born with halters round their necks." This is the line that tossed Pip overboard, entangled Fedallah, slew Ahab. Complementary to this death-line is the life-line, the "monkey-rope" that ties seamen together. "So that for better or for worse, we two, for the time, were wedded; and should poor Queequeg sink to rise no more, then both usage and honor demanded that instead of cutting the cord, it should drag me down in its wake. So, then, an elongated Simaese ligature united us." The life-line is at once a love-link, a death-line, and an umbilicus. These cords are intermingled again as the harpooner's line tangles with the trailing umbilicus of new-born whale cubs. Love and death are imaged together when Ishmael regards the whale-line in its tub as "a prodigious wedding-cake to present to the whales." Even the weather contributes to the loomed design as "mingling threads of life are woven by warp and woof; calm crossed by storm, a storm for every calm.... Where lies the final harbor, whence we unmoor no more?"

That final harbor is as hidden from mortal navigators as the "insular Tahiti" of unfallen delight, once pushed off from never to be found again. Yet Pip has moored there. For when afloat on the terrifying sea "He saw God's foot upon the treadle of the loom, and spoke it.... So man's insanity is heaven's sense; and wandering from all mortal reason, man comes at last to that celestial thought, which, to reason, is absurd and frantic; and weal or woe, feels then uncompromised, indifferent as his God."[5]

Indifferent, that is, to mortal weal or woe; these are no concern of the God who set down "WHALING VOYAGE BY ONE ISHMAEL" in "the grand programme of Providence that was drawn up a long time ago." For that God—Ishmael's God—is himself creative power, subsuming all the fragmentary deities men erect in his partial image: Ahab's and Fedallah's destructive Force, Queequeg's all-fructifying love, Pip's and Bulkington's Christian Absolute, the Divine Inert. Transcending the sum of these is the ever-emergent God of Life and Death, revealing Himself through Nature, the Work that he creates. Moby Dick, the greatest of his handiwork, is the principle of Godhead *in* Nature. This God does not allow (as Richard Chase among others reminds us) either a tragic or a Christian resolution of man's fate; Melville's view does indeed resemble at some points Spinoza's (as Newton Arvin has suggested), that man's happiness consists in knowing his true place in nature. Far more deeply than the literary naturalists of the end of his century, he comprehends in the cosmos a God of energy whose moral laws, if they exist, transcend all human divination. Yet Melville's God of Force is not like Zola's or Dreiser's or Crane's, Himself a mere machine; in *Moby-Dick* that view is Ahab's blindness. Melville posits not immutable mechanical law but the universal vitality of Nature, embracing death as preludial to rebirth. In this he comes close to Whitman, though Melville cannot rest as easily as Whitman did with the facile and unstable resolution of all dilemmas proposed in "Song of Myself."

[5]Ahab saw *his* pattern too, "when God's burning finger [was] laid upon the ship; when His 'Mene, Tekel, Upharsin' [was] woven into the shrouds and cordage." Then Ahab embraced the corpusants, as though to knot the design against the unraveling of chance.

As close as Melville comes to a resolution in *Moby-Dick* is in a chapter few critics have noticed, "A Bower in the Arsacides." Here the images of the white whale and the weaver-god come together in Ishmael's mind, and here too is the image of the machine—indeed, a modern industrial factory. Such images define the limits of Ahab's will, for his "path...is laid with iron rails, whereon [his] soul is grooved to run"; but here Ishmael sees the mechanical in its right relation to cosmic truth. These images of whale, weaver, and machine occur in Ishmael's mind as he recalls a previous voyage when he visited the island where a whale's white skeleton forms a chapel decked with vines. This is a context independent of both Ahab, his own crippling death-wish, and Queequeg, his own regressive infantilism. One last extended excerpt will repay our consideration:

> The industrious earth beneath was as a weaver's loom, with a gorgeous carpet on it, whereof the ground-fine tendrils formed the warp and woof, and the living flowers the figures.... Through the lacings of the leaves, the great sun seemed a flying shuttle weaving the unwearied verdure. Oh, busy weaver!—pause!—one word!— whither flows the fabric? what palace may it deck? wherefore all these ceaseless toilings? Speak, weaver!—stay thy hand!—but one single word with thee! Nay—the shuttle flies—the figures float from forth the loom; the freshet-rushing carpet for ever slides away. The weaver-god, he weaves; and by that weaving is he deafened, that he hears no mortal voice; and by that humming we, too, who look on the loom are deafened; and only when we escape it shall we hear the thousand voices that speak through it. For even so it is in all material factories. The spoken words that are inaudible among the flying spindles; those same words are plainly heard without the walls, bursting from the opened casements. Ah, mortal! then, be heedful; for so, in all this din of the great world's loom, thy subtlest thinkings may be overheard afar.
>
> Now, amid the green, life-restless loom of that Arsacidean wood, the great, white, worshipped skeleton lay lounging—a gigantic idler. Yet...the mighty idler seemed the cunning weaver; himself all woven over with vines...but himself a skeleton. Life folded Death; Death trellised Life; the grim god wived with youthful Life, and begat him curly-headed glories.

Here process is mechanical; in the mortal activity of becoming, the Word is drowned. That activity is only the effect, not the Source, of divine energy. The skeleton whale—white—"seemed the cunning weaver"—for on this island as well as on the *Pequod's* ocean (and in Job) we can come no nearer to the Source than to behold the greatest of His works. It is the loom of this whale's dead bones, interwoven with life, that Ishmael measured with a ball of twine and tattooed upon his own right arm.

How then can we stand beyond the walls of the factory to hear the Word that its mechanical humming drowns? How fathom the pattern in the endless fabric of Life and Death? One way is amply plain—by stepping outside of the world of process, we, with the death of our human senses, may behold the grand design. But Ishmael at last will be redeemed from such a Redemption. He wills himself to *live*. And what truth he has survived to tell us we may find written on the whale's brow, "pleated with riddles." These are unriddled on the whale's talisman, the doubloon.

On that coin "the keystone sun" came through the zodiac at "the equinoctal point of Libra," the scales. And the coin was made in Ecuador, "a country planted in the middle of the world," named for the equator, and was minted "in the unwaning clime that knows no autumn." None of these visible facts had been *felt* by any of the doubloon's beholders; each save Pip sought the phantom of life and grasped only "his own mysterious self." Pip, already at the Resurrection, is beyond the doubloon's gift of wisdom, which Ishmael alone receives.

The scales of Libra are no doubt those "scales of the New Testament" by which Ishmael weighed his mortal lot at the beginning and found it tolerable. What is important here is that at *their* point in the heavens the "keystone sun" enters the universe. But the conception of balance is not only transcendent; represented by the pagan zodiac, the geographic equator, and the physical reality of that "unwaning clime" halfway up the Andes, the idea necessarily extends to *that wholeness which is comprised of both the halves:* both hemispheres, both peaks and valleys, both winter and summer, both hot and cold—both love and death, highest good and deepest evil, mortality and immortality. Unlike Starbuck's *mediocritas,* this balanced, doubled vision encompasses all extremes and thereby asserts its absolute stability. It is godlike. To attain it and survive, Ishmael must drown his Ahab and his Queequeg. But first he must have acknowledged them.

Like the builders of the Cathedral of Cologne, Melville leaves the true copestone of *Moby-Dick* to posterity. Had he imposed perfect form upon his partial vision of the truth he sought, he would have falsified his own achievement. This is an intrinsic principle of Melville's aesthetic. Yet in *Moby-Dick* the incandescence of the metaphoric linkage we have observed does project successfully the unification of experience. It does this by creating autonomously the world within which its own meanings are true. This world is braced and pinioned by the primitive sanctions and mythic values, the supernatural forces and ritualistic acts that we have traced. And yet, as distant as such materials would seem to be from the workaday life of Melville's time, in *Moby-Dick* he elaborates almost all of the levels of experience, as well as of mythic feeling and metaphoric thought, which might typify his culture and his time. From savagery to spindle-factories, from Old Testament Calvinism to the gamecocks of the frontier, from demonology to capitalism, the imagery of American life on every level sinews the entire book. Melville's view of life is doubtless a less catholic view than we find in Dante, or in his favorite author Shakespeare, or in Cervantes. Yet his is the greatest work by an American imagination for the same reasons that theirs are the greatest works of European Christendom. *Moby-Dick* most profoundly expresses the aspirations and the limitations of the culture as well as the individual genius that produced it. And that culture has, thus far, given us fewer tragic heroes and transcendent Christians than individualists alienated from their pasts, striving to discover those "humanities" which yet may bind them to "the magnetic circle of mankind."

Moby-Dick as Poetic Epic

by Lewis Mumford

Moby-Dick is a poetic epic. Typographically, Moby-Dick conforms to prose, and there are long passages, whole chapters, which are wholly in the mood of prose: but in spirit and in actual rhythm, Moby-Dick again and again rises to polyphonic verse which resembles passages of Webster's in that it can either be considered as broken blank verse, or as cadenced prose. Mr. Percy Boynton has performed the interesting experiment of transposing a paragraph in Pierre into excellent free verse, so strong and subtle are Melville's rhythms; and one might garner a whole book of verse from Moby-Dick. Melville, in Moby-Dick, unconsciously respects Poe's canon that all true poetry must be short in length, since the mood cannot be retained, unbroken or undiminished, over lengthy passages, and if the form itself is preserved, the content nevertheless is prose. But while Poe himself used this dictum as an excuse for writing only short lyrics, Melville sustained the poetic mood through a long narrative by dropping frankly into prose in the intervening while. As a result, he was under no necessity of clipping the emotions or of bleaching the imaginative colours of Moby-Dick: like a flying-boat, he rises from the water to the air and returns to the water again without losing control over either medium. His prose is prose: hard, senewy, compact; and his poetry is poetry, vivid, surging, volcanic, creating its own form in the very pattern of the emotional state itself, soaring, towering, losing all respect for the smaller conventions of veracity, when the inner triumph itself must be announced. It is in the very rhythm of his language that Ahab's mood, and all the devious symbols of Moby-Dick are sustained and made credible: by no other method could the deeper half of the tale have been written. In these poetic passages, the phrases are intensified, stylicized, stripped of their habitual associations. If occasionally, as with Shakespeare, the thought itself is borne down by the weight of the gold that decorates it, this is only a similar proof of Melville's immense fecundity of expression.

Both Poe and Hawthorne share some of Melville's power, and both of them, with varying success, wrought ideality and actuality into the same figure: but one has only to compare the best of their work with *Moby-Dick* to see wherein Melville's great distinction lies. *The Scarlet Letter, The House of the Seven Gables, William Wilson*, like most other works of fiction, are melodic: a single instrument is sufficient to carry the whole theme; whereas *Moby-Dick* is a symphony; every resource of language and thought, fantasy, description, philosophy, natural history, drama, broken rhythms, blank verse, imagery, symbol, is utilized to sustain and expand the great theme. The conception of *Moby-Dick* organically demands the expressive interrelation, for a single total effect, of a hundred different pieces: even in accessory matters, like the association of the Parsee, the fire-worshipper, with the death of Ahab, the fire-defier, or in the makeup of the crew, the officers white men, the harpooners the savage races, red, black, brown, and the crew a mixed lot from the separate islands of the earth, not a stroke is introduced that has not a meaning for the myth as a whole. Although the savage harpooners get nearest the whale, the savage universe, it is Ahab and the Parsee, the Westerner and the Asiatic, who carry the pursuit to its ultimate end—while a single American survives to tell the tale!

Melville's instrumentation is unsurpassed in the writing of the last century: one must go to a Beethoven or a Wagner for an exhibition of similar powers: one will not find it among the works of literature. Here are Webster's wild violin, Marlowe's cymbals, Browne's sonorous bass viol, Swift's brass, Smollett's castanets, Shelley's flute, brought together in a single orchestra, complementing each other in a grand symphony. Melville achieved a similar synthesis in thought; and that work has proved all the more credible because he achieved it in language, too. Small wonder that those who were used to elegant pianoforte solos or barrel-organ instrumentation, were deafened and surprised and repulsed.

What is the meaning of *Moby-Dick*? There is not one meaning; there are many; but in its simplest terms, *Moby-Dick* is, necessarily, a story of the sea and its ways, as the *Odyssey* is a story of strange adventure, and *War and Peace* a story of battles and domestic life. The characters are heightened and slightly distorted: Melville's quizzical comic sense, not unakin to Thoreau's, is steadily at work on them, and only Ahab escapes: but they all have their recognizable counterparts in the actual world. Without any prolonged investigation one could still find a Starbuck on Nantucket or a Flask on Martha's Vineyard—indeed, as Mr. Thomas Benton's portraits properly indicate, queerer fish than they.

On this level, *Moby-Dick* brings together and focusses in a single picture the long line of sketches and preliminary portraits Melville had assembled in *Typee, Omoo, Redburn,* and *White-Jacket.* As a story of the sea, *Moby-Dick* will always have a call for those who wish to recapture the magic and terror and stress and calm delight of the sea and its ships; and not less so because it seizes on a particular kind of ship, the whaler, and a special occupation, whaling, at the moment when they were about to pass out of existence, or rather, were being transformed from a brutal but glorious battle into a methodical, somewhat banal industry. Melville had the singular fortune to pronounce a valedictory on many ways of life and scenes that were becoming extinct. He lived among the South Sea Islanders when they were still pretty much as Captain Cook found them, just before their perversion and decimation by our exotic Western civilization. He recorded life on a man-of-war half a generation before the sail gave place to steam, wood to armour-plate, and grappling-irons to long-range guns. He described life on a sailing-packet before steam had increased the speed, the safety, and the pleasant monotony of transatlantic travel: and finally, he recorded the last heroic days of whaling. *Moby-Dick* would have value as first-hand testimony, even if it were negligible as literature. If this were all, the book would still be important.

But *Moby-Dick,* admirable as it is as a narrative of maritime adventure, is far more than that: it is, fundamentally, a parable on the mystery of evil and the accidental malice of the universe. On one reading, the white whale stands for the brute energies of existence, blind, fatal, overpowering, while Ahab is the spirit of man, small and feeble, but purposeful, that pits its puniness against this might, and its purpose against the blank senselessness of power. The evil arises with the good: the white whale grows up among the milder whales which are caught and cut up and used: one hunts for the one—for a happy marriage, livelihood, offspring, social companionship and cheer—and suddenly heaving its white bulk out of the calm sea, one comes upon the other: illness, accident, treachery, jealousy, vengefulness, dull frustration. The South Sea savage did not know of the white whale: at least, like death, it played but a casual part in his consciousness. It is different with the European: his life is a torment of white whales: the Jobs, the Aeschyluses, the Dantes, the Shakespeares, pursue him and grapple with him, as Ahab pursues his antagonist.

All our lesser literature, all our tales of Avalon or Heaven or ultimate redemption, or, in a later day, the Future, is an evasion of the white whale: it is a quest of that boyish beginning which we call a happy ending. But the old Norse myth told that Asgard itself would be consumed at last, and the very gods would be destroyed: the white whale is the symbol of that persistent force of destruction, that meaningless force, which now figures as the outpouring of a volcano or the atmospheric disruption of a tornado or again as the mere aimless dissipation of unused energy into an unavailable void—that spectacle which so disheartened the learned Henry Adams. The whole tale of the West, in mind and action, in the moral wrestlings of the Jews, in the philosophy and art of the Greeks, in the organization and technique of the Romans, in the precise skills and unceasing spiritual quests of the modern man, is a tale of this effort to combat the whale—to ward off his blows, to counteract his aimless thrusts, to create a purpose that will offset the empty malice of Moby Dick. Without such a purpose, without the belief in such a purpose, life is neither bearable nor significant: unless one is fortified by these central human energies and aims, one tends to become absorbed in Moby Dick himself, and, becoming a part of his being, can only maim, slay, butcher, like the shark or the white whale or Alexander or Napoleon. If there is no God, exclaims Dostoyevsky's hero, then we may commit murder: and in the sense that God represents the totality of human value, meaning, and transcendent possibility the conclusion is inevitable.

It is useless to reduce man's purposes to those of the id; he is a figure in the whole web of life. Except for such kindness and loyalty as the creatures man has domesticated show, there is, as

far as one can now see, no concern except in man himself over
the ceaseless motions and accidents that take place in nature.
Love and chance, said Charles Peirce, rule the universe: but that
love is fitful, and although in the very concept of chance, as both
Peirce and Captain Ahab declare, there is some rough notion of
fair play, of fifty-fifty, of an even break, that is small immediate
consolation for the creature that may lose not the game, but his
life, by an unlucky throw of the dice. Ahab has more humanity
than the gods he defies: indeed, he has more power, because he
is conscious of the power he wields, and applies it deliberately,
whereas Moby Dick's power only seems deliberate because it cuts
across the directed aims of Ahab himself. And in one sense, Ahab
achieves victory: he vanquishes in himself that which would retreat from Moby Dick and acquiesce in his insensate energies and
his brutal sway. His end is tragic: evil engulfs him. But in battling
against evil, with power instead of love, Ahab himself, in A. E.'s
phrase, becomes the image of the thing he hates: he has lost his
humanity in the very act of vindicating it. By physical defiance,
by physical combat, Ahab cannot rout and capture Moby Dick:
the odds are against him; and if his defiance is noble, his final
aim is confessedly mad. Cultivation, order, art—these are the
proper means by which man displaces accident and subdues the
vacant external powers in the universe: the way of growth is not
to become more powerful but to become more human.

Here is a hard lesson to learn: it is easier to wage war than to
conquer in oneself the tendency to be partial, vindictive, and unjust: it is easier to demolish one's enemy than to pit oneself against
him in an intellectual combat which will disclose one's weaknesses
and provincialities. And that shapeless evil Ahab seeks to strike
is the sum of one's enemies. He does not bow down to it and accept it: therein lie his heroism and virtue: but he fights it with
its own weapons and therein lies his madness. All the things that
Ahab despises when he is about to attack the whale, the love and
loyalty of Pip, the memory of his wife and child, the sextant of
science, the inner sense of calm, which makes all external struggle
futile, are the very things that would redeem him and make him
victorious.

Man's ultimate defence against the Universe, against evil and
accident and malice, is not by any fictitious resolution of these
things into an Absolute which justifies them and utilizes them for
its own ends: this is specious comfort, and Voltaire's answer to

Leibniz in *Candide* seems to me a final one. Man's defence lies within himself, not within the narrow, isolated ego, which may be overwhelmed, but in that social self which we share with our fellows and which assures us that, whatever happens to our own carcasses and hides, good men will remain, to carry on the work, to foster and protect the things we have recognized as excellent. To make that self more solid, one must advance positive science, produce formative ideas, and embody ideal forms in which all men may, to a greater or less degree, participate—in short must create a realm which is independent of the insensate forces in the universe—and cannot be lightly shaken by their onslaught. Melville's method, that of writing *Moby-Dick,* was correct: as correct as Ahab's method, taken literally, that of fighting Moby Dick, was fallacious.

In the very creation of *Moby-Dick,* Melville conquered the white whale that threatened him: instead of horror there was significance, instead of aimless energy there was purpose, and instead of random power there was meaningful life. The universe *is* inscrutable, unfathomable, overwhelming—like the white whale and his element. Art in the broad sense of all humanizing effort is man's answer to this condition: for it is the means by which he circumvents or postpones his doom, transcends his creaturely limitations, and bravely meets his tragic destiny.

Metaphor and Language in *Moby-Dick*

by Newton Arvin

The imagery of armies and of warfare...is recurrent in *Moby-Dick,* and for evident reasons. It keeps us from forgetting that butchery and carnage are close to the center of the theme, yet it lifts even them to a level on which the imagination can accept them. In general, however, the metaphors—and the allusions that have a quasi-metaphorical role—point in two opposite directions and, as a result, enhance the duality of tone that is so profound an aspect of the book's character. There are the metaphors that, like some of the similes, ennoble and aggrandize the texture of the narrative; and there are those that, like others, diminish or subdue it or even make it humorous. On the one hand, we are repeatedly put in mind of royalty or imperial dignity, of Czars and Sultans, or of the great figures of legend or history (Perseus, Alexander, the Crusaders, Tamerlane) or of Biblical story. Some of the most profound intuitions, moreover, are embodied in metaphors of architectural or monumental grandeur (the ruins of Lima, "the great dome of St. Peter's," the halls of Thermes below the Hôtel de Cluny) or in metaphors of naturalistic power and beauty ("the unabated Hudson," "one insular Tahiti," "the flame Baltic of Hell," or, perhaps most memorably of all, the meadows under the slopes of the Andes). All this is true, but it is also true that there is a constant contrapuntal play of shrunken or diminishing metaphors, and that these have a decidedly Shakesperean or at any rate Elizabethan rather than an epic quality, as when Ahab hoots at the gods as mere pugilists and cricket-players, or "Death himself" is likened to a postboy, or a Sperm Whale and his spout are compared to a portly burgher smoking his pipe of a warm afternoon. Close to these in feeling are the images that come from

"Metaphor and Language in *Moby-Dick*" [editor's title] by Newton Arvin. From *Herman Melville,* by Newton Arvin (New York: William Sloane Associates, Inc., 1950), pp. 160-65. Copyright © 1950 by William Sloane Associates, Inc. Reprinted by permission of William Morrow & Co., Inc.

nineteenth-century industry or technology, the images of drilling and blasting, of mining, of cogged wheels and mechanical looms and magnetic wires, and even the "Leyden jar" of Ahab's "own magnetic life."

These latter metaphors are not without a suggestion of some of the metaphysical poets or of twentieth-century poetry; at other points in *Moby-Dick* one is reminded, by the constant recurrence of imagery from animal life, of *Lear* and *Timon* on the one hand and on the other of Melville's contemporaries, the naturalistic novelists, Balzac and Zola. The Sperm Whale of course is one of the great primary symbols, and actual creatures of the sea, squid and sharks and swordfish, appear not as metaphors but as secondary symbols. In addition to these, however, which are given by the very subject, almost the whole range of animal life, wild and domestic, seems to have been scoured for images. Ahab himself is likened to a tiger, to a grizzly bear, to a wolf, a moose, a sea-lion, a walrus; and Pip even calls him "that anaconda of an old man." There is a steady, stately parade of elephants throughout the book; these greatest of land beasts are deliberately evoked as attendants, so to say, upon the greatest animal of the sea. The pagan harpooners and the Parsees are sometimes, like Ahab, compared to tigers, and in the famous chapter on "The Whiteness of the Whale" everyone will remember the polar bear, the unspottedly white albatross, the sacred White Dog of the Iroquois, and the spectral White Steed of the Prairies. And indeed, as these allusions suggest, there is both a likeness and a difference between Melville's animal metaphors and either Shakespeare's or Balzac's. It is true that, like those writers (in their wholly dissimilar ways), he sometimes intends to suggest an analogy between the ferocity or the bestiality of men and that of beasts; but Melville's intention is more ambiguous than theirs, and it is quite as much for the sake of imparting to his theme a certain majesty, a certain grandeur, a certain strangeness of beauty, that he introduces his often splendid animals and birds.

Certainly nothing could be more eloquent of the incandescence out of which *Moby-Dick* was written than the variety and the idiosyncrasy of the metaphors with which it is animated; nothing, perhaps, except the equally extraordinary resourcefulness and inventiveness of Melville's language. For this there is nothing in his earlier books to prepare us fully, though there are hints of it in the best passages of *Redburn* and *White-Jacket*. In general,

however, the diction in those books is the current diction of good
prose in Melville's time; it has a hardly definable personal quality. Now, in *Moby-Dick*, it takes on abruptly an idiosyncrasy of
the most unmistakable sort; it is a question now of Melvillean
language in the same intense and special sense in which one
speaks of Virgilian language, of Shakesperean, or Miltonic. It
is a creation, verbally speaking; a great artifice; a particular
characterizing idiom; without it the book would not exist. One of
its hallmarks, as in all the other cases, is the "signature" furnished
by favorite words; the favorite nouns, adjectives, and adverbs
that end by coloring the fabric of the book as strongly as the use
of a favorite range of hues affects the manner of a painter. Like
Virgil, with his *pius, ingens,* and *immanis,* or Shakespeare, with
his *rich, brave, sweet,* and *gentle,* Melville has his own verbal
palette: it is chiefly made up of the words *wild, wildly,* and *wild-
ness, moody* and *moodiness* ("moody Ahab," especially), *mystic*
and *mystical, subtle, subtly,* and *subtlety, wondrous* ("most wondrous philosophies"), *nameless, intense,* and *malicious*
("malicious agencies"). One has only to cite these words to suggest how intimately expressive they are of *Moby-Dick's* dark,
violent, and enigmatic theme.

It is a matter, however, not only of characteristic words, familiar
in themselves to readers of Melville's time and ours, but of characteristic *kinds* of words and of words that are again and again his
own coinages or at least of a great rarity. One feels, as in all such
cases, that the limits of even the English vocabulary have suddenly begun to seem too strict, too penurious, and that the dif-'
ficult things Melville has to say can be adequately said only by
reaching beyond those limits. He does so, perhaps most strikingly, in the constant use he makes of verbal nouns, mostly in the
plural, and usually his own inventions; such nouns, for example,
as *regardings, allurings, intercedings, wanings, coincidings,* and
the nouns one gets in the strangely connotative phrases, "nameless
invisible *domineerings"* and "such lovely *leewardings."* Almost
unanalyzable is the effect these have on uniting the dynamism of
the verb and the stasis of the substantive. And so of the other abstract
nouns Melville loves to use in the plural—*defilements, tran-
quillities, unfulfilments,* "sorrow's *technicals,"* and "unshored,
harborless *immensities."* In their very unliteral pluralized form
these characteristic abstractions become an elusive kind of in-

verted metaphor. Very different and less metaphorical, but almost as special in their effect, are the nouns Melville habitually constructs with the suffix *-ness (localness, landlessness, aborigalness, inter-indebtedness)* or *-ism (footmanism, sultanism, Titanism,* and the Carlylean *vultureism).*

Quite as abundant as the unfamiliar nouns are the unfamiliar adjectives and adverbs that do so much to give the style of *Moby-Dick* its particular unconformable character. And again, just as verbal nouns are Melville's most characteristic substantives, so adjectives and adverbs based on present or past participles are his most characteristic modifiers; participial adjectives such as *officered, cymballed, omnitooled, unensanguined, uncatastrophied,* "last, *cindered* apple" and "*stumped* and *paupered* arm"; and participial adverbs such as *invokingly, intermixingly, gallopingly, suckingly, postponedly,* and *uninterpenetratingly.* These however are only the most characteristic of his modifiers; a complete list would have to include such rarities as *unsmoothable, familyless, spermy, flavorish, leviathanic,* and *unexempt* (which might have echoed in his mind from *Comus)* or (for adverbs) *diagonically, Spanishly, Venetianly,* and *sultanically.* And even beyond these one would have to glance at the sometimes odd, sometimes magnificent compounds, almost always adjectival, that give so vibrating a life to the pages of the book: "a *valor-ruined* man," "the *message-carrying* air," "the *circus-running* sun," "*teeth-tiered* sharks," and "*god-bullied* hull." There is an energy of verbal inventiveness here that it is hardly too much to call Aeschylean or Shakesperean.

It does not, curiously, express itself in the formation of unfamiliar verbs so typically as in these other ways; this is a kind of anomaly in a style of which the capacity to evoke movement, action, and all kinds of kinaesthetic sensations is so great. Melville, indeed, uses familiar or not unfamiliar verbs, again and again, with beautiful force; yet the impulsion of some of his finest passages of vehement action depends only partly on these; it depends at least as much on other parts of speech, as a characteristic paragraph such as this will suggest:

A short rushing sound leaped out of the boat; it was the darted iron of Queequeg. Then all in one welded commotion came an invisible push from astern, while forward the boat seemed striking on a ledge; the sail collapsed and exploded; a gush of scalding vapor shot up near by; something rolled and tumbled like an earthquake beneath us. The whole crew were half suffocated as they were tossed helter-skelter into the white curdling cream of the squall....

Nothing could be finer than a sound leaping out of a boat, or than the "something" that "rolled and tumbled beneath us," but the effect of the passage obviously depends on the vigor with which quite ordinary verbs are used, and at least as much on the vitality of the nouns and adjectives ("welded commotion," "invisible push"). Only rarely, but then sometimes with irresistible effect, does Melville create his own verbs, or virtually create them: "who didst *thunder* him higher than a throne," "he *tasks* me, he *heaps* me," "my fingers...began...to *serpentine* and *spiralize*," and "skies the most effulgent but *basket* the deadliest thunders." In all these cases, of course, he has boldly made verbs out of nouns or adjectives; and indeed, from this point of view, the manner in which the parts of speech are "intermixingly" assorted in Melville's style—so that the distinction between verbs and nouns, substantives and modifiers, becomes a half unreal one —this is the prime characteristic of his language. No feature of it could express more tellingly the awareness that lies below and behind *Moby-Dick*—the awareness that action and condition, movement and stasis, object and idea, are but surface aspects of one underlying reality.

Queequeg: The Well-Governed Shark

by Robert Zoellner

The full meaning of this frightful sharkishness in Ishmael's "bosom friend" does not come clear...until almost halfway through *Moby-Dick* when Fleece, the *Pequod's* black cook, delivers his homily to the sharks. This second sermon, in many respects contrapuntal to Father Mapple's sermon on Jonah, establishes the philosophical and moral parameters requisite for a true understanding of Queequeg's significance. When, at midnight, Stubb's whale-steak supper is disturbed by the mastications of thousands upon thousands of sharks swarming about the dead whale lashed to the ship's side, the petulant second mate orders old Fleece to "preach to 'em!" in the hope that decorum will be restored. Opening on an appropriately pastoral note, Fleece addresses the sharks as "Belubed fellow-critters":

> Dough you is all sharks, and by natur wery woracious, yet I zay to you, fellow-critters, dat dat woraciousness—'top dat dam slappin' ob de tail! How you tink to hear, 'spose you keep up such a dam slappin' and bitin' dare? [Here a profane remonstrance from Stubb on profanity, and then the sermon continues.] Your woraciousness, fellow-critters, I don't blame ye so much for; dat is natur, and can't be helped; but to gobern dat wicked natur, dat is de pint. You is sharks, sartin; but if you gobern de shark in you, why den you be angel; for all angel is not'ing more dan de shark well goberned. Now, look here, bred'ren, just try wonst to be cibil, a helping yourselbs from dat whale. Don't be tearin' de blubber out your neighbour's mout, I say. Is not one shark dood right as toder to dat whale? And, by Gor, none on you has de right to dat whale; dat whale belong to some one else. I know some o' you has berry brig mout, brigger dan oders; but den de brig mouts sometimes has de

"Queequeg: The Well-Governed Shark" by Robert Zoellner. From *The Salt-Sea Mastodon: A Reading of Moby-Dick* by Robert Zoellner (Berkeley and Los Angeles: The University of California Press, 1973), pp. 219-25. Copyright © 1973 by the Regents of the University of California; reprinted by permission of the University of California Press.

small bellies; so dat the brigness ob de mout is not to swallar wid,
but to bite off de blubber for de small fry ob sharks, dat can't get
into de scrouge to help demselves. (64: *250-51)*[1]

Over a century after Melville wrote these lines, one can only feel
embarrassment at such evidence—pervasive in nineteenth-
century American literature from Fenimore Cooper on—that
possession of moral sensitivity and high creative gifts does not
necessarily arm one against the prejudices and stereotypical
thinking of one's culture. Melville's conception of the black personality in *Moby-Dick*—and most especially in Pip and Fleece—
must be a source of chagrin to all twentieth-century readers. But
revulsion at this tasteless attempt to draw on the crude traditions
of "darky" humor should not prevent us from seeing that Melville is being crude with a purpose. For the fact is that the black
pseudo-dialect of Fleece's sermon is a deliberate mask. All one has
to do is rewrite the sermon in "straight" English to see that we are
in actuality dealing with someone other than a sleepy ship's cook.

The tip-off is the word *voracious,* masked as *woracious.* Every
other character in *Moby-Dick* speaks according to his station and
background. Ahab has been to college as well as among the cannibals; Ishmael is a bookish ex-schoolmaster; Starbuck is deeply
read in the Bible—and all three speak in a manner commensurate
with these facts. Stubb and Flask speak the rough-and-ready idiom
one expects from subordinate ship's officers. Queequeg, Tashtego, and Daggoo likewise express themselves in locutions re-
flecting their wild vitality. But this correlation breaks down with
Fleece. Not only does the old man employ bookish adjectives
such as *voracious* and *civil,* and learned verbs such as *to govern.* He
also manages, in the compass of some twenty lines, to touch upon
the issues of the *nature of life,* the place of *government,* the need
for *civility,* the question of *inherent rights,* the sanctity of *private
property,* the demands of *charity,* the problem of *equality,* the
source and nature of *good and evil,* and the moral relationship of
the *strong to the weak.* This is an astonishing midnight perfor-
mance for a half-awake cook on a lowly American whaler. Fleece,
it seems clear, is mouthing somebody else's words. It is equally

[1]Citations to *Moby-Dick* are from the Norton Critical Edition, ed. Harrison
Hayford and Hershel Parker (New York: W. W. Norton & Co., 1967). The number before the colon indicates chapter; the italicized numbers after the colon
indicate page [editor's note].

clear that the "somebody else" is Melville himself. The old cook's sermon is perhaps the only place in *Moby-Dick* where, for a certainty, the mind of Melville himself can be detected moving beneath the dense web of the textual surface. Fleece's synthetic dialect represents a not-very-successful attempt to construct a verbal screen of maximum opacity, a diversionary mask to hide the sudden and unprecedented presence of the author in the fictional world he has created. Such an analysis prevents us from dismissing Fleece, as Warner Berthoff does, as a mere "figure of fun."[2] Fleece represents instead a unique instance of auctorial intrusion into an otherwise hermetic fictional world. As such, his sermon demands that close attention reserved for unique literary events.

The importance of what Fleece has to say lies in the differing reactions which Ishmael and the *Pequod*'s cook exhibit when confronted with the fact of sharkishness. When Ishmael gazes over the side at the thousands of sharks insensately tearing head-sized chunks of blubber out of Stubb's whale, he speaks despairingly of *devils*. When, less than a page later, Fleece lowers a lantern and contemplates the same scene, he speaks of *angels*. This shift from devil to angel schematizes a major resolution in *Moby-Dick*. But the precise nature of that resolution cannot be established until another and quite distinct level of meaning is disentangled from Fleece's rambling monologue. This is the level on which Fleece's sermon can be read as a commentary on Father Mapple's. Jonah's story is a tale of "the sin, hard-heartedness, suddenly awakened fears, the swift punishment, repentance, prayers, and finally the deliverance and joy of Jonah." The prophet's sin is "wilful disobedience of the command of God." "And if we obey God," Father Mapple asserts, "we must disobey ourselves; and it is in this disobeying ourselves, wherein the hardness of obeying God consists" (9: *45*). Self-disobedience, then, is the norm of Father Mapple's Christian universe. Jonah is not persuaded to do God's bidding. Rather, he is forced to—forced, that is, to disobey himself. Overwhelmed by the "hard hand of God," he becomes "aghast Jonah," reduced to "cringing attitudes" (9: *48*). As with Jonah, so with the ship's crew. When they pity him, refusing to cast him overboard, "seek[ing] by other means to save the ship," God simply increases the intensity of the storm until

[2] *The Example of Melville* (Princeton: Princeton University Press, 1962), pp. 106, 178.

the crew disobey their charitable instincts and throw Jonah over
the side (9: *49*). Father Mapple's version of the Christian message
demands, in short, that we go against our own natures and deny
our own humanity. It is Augustinian and Calvinist Christianity,
that same Stylitic tradition which, over the centuries, has persuaded some men to suppress their sexuality, some to abort their
natural talents, others to withdraw into monastic isolation, and
still others to flagellate their living flesh.

Put in these terms—man's relationship to his own human nature
—the connection between Father Mapple's sermon and Fleece's
sermon becomes immediately apparent. Fleece deals explicitly
with the *nature* of the living, responding creature. He begins by
reminding the blood-lusting rabble over the *Pequod's* side that
"you is all sharks, and by natur wery woracious." Interrupted by
Stubb, he resumes by making the same point again. "Your woraciousness, fellow-critters, I don't blame ye so much for; dat is
natur, and can't be helped." Having twice asserted the intracta-
bility of "natur," Fleece then proves his thesis by urging the
principal imperatives of Christian civilization upon his congregation. They should, for example, try to be civil, learning to love
one another: "Now, look here, bred'ren, just try wonst to be
cibil....Don't be tearin' de blubber out your neighbour's mout,
I say." He urges them to be sensitive to each other's rights: "Is
not one shark dood right as toder [as good a right as another] to
dat whale?" The sharks should also recognize the prior rights of
possession and private ownership: "And, by Gor, none on you
has de right to dat whale; dat whale belong to someone else."
Above all, Fleece pleads for charity and the golden rule, especially
as these apply to the strong and the gifted: "I know some o' you
has berry brig mout, brigger dan oders;...de brigness ob de mout
is not to swallar wid, but to bite off de blubber for de small fry ob
sharks." In short, in an unmistakable parody of Father Mapple's
view of man, Fleece asks the sharks to "disobey themselves," to go
against their own sharkish natures. He asks them to suppress, or
more precisely, *extirpate* their own sharkishness. He asks them to
stop being sharks. Lest we miss the point, Stubb makes it explicit.
"Well done, old Fleece!" he exclaims, "that's Christianity" (64:
251). But Fleece's homily is, on this level, an exercise in futility:

> No use goin' on; de dam willains will keep a scrougin' and slap-
> pin' each oder, Massa Stubb; dey don't hear one word; no use a-

preachin' to such dam g'uttons as you call 'em, till dare bellies is full, and dare bellies is bottomless; and when dey do get 'em full, dey wont hear you den; for den dey sink in de sea, go fast to sleep on de coral, and can't hear not'ing at all, no more, for eber and eber. (64: *251-52*).

The meaning is clear; it is utterly hopeless to urge sharks to stop being sharks—or men to stop being men. Moral and ethical imperatives which demand the suppression, the distortion, or (most especially) the *extirpation* of essential nature can lead only to alienation from self and hypocrisy toward others.

But Fleece delivers his sermon not only to the finny and aqueous sharks over the *Pequod's* side. Standing at his shoulder to hear the exhortation is Stubb, a human shark who likes his steak blood-rare, but who in this respect is no different from Queequeg and Peleg and Bildad and Ahab, and indeed the entire crew of the *Pequod*— all of them, as Starbuck has it, "Whelped somewhere by the sharkish sea" (38: *148*). What Fleece has to say applies even to ex-schoolmaster Ishmael, who despite his bookish mildness, admits that "I myself am a savage, owning no allegiance but to the King of the Cannibals; and ready at any moment to rebel against him" (57: *232*). For these bipedal and terrestrial sharks, Fleece introduces the idea of control, of *government*. This level of the sermon is signaled by the old man's addressing his congregation as "Belubed fellow-critters," and, a little later, as "bred'ren." Fleece speaks thus to Brother Shark because he knows that Stubb, and all of us, share with these most insensately vicious monsters of the deep a hankering taste for the carnivorous and the ensanguined. The whole sermon is on this level deeply ironic, darkly tinged with an inverted and demonic Franciscanism. For the oceanic sharks any degree of self-government is obviously out of the question. The failure of the sermon to produce the quiet and decorum which Stubb demands is proof enough of that. But Fleece's *human* "fellow-critters" are another matter. "Your woraciousness, fellow-critters;...is natur, and can't be helped; but to gobern dat wicked natur, dat is de pint. You is sharks, sartin; but if you gobern de shark in you, why den you be angel; for all angel is not'ing more dan de shark well goberned" (64: *251*).

Nothing could be more startling than this abrupt introduction of the idea of the *angelic* into Fleece's dark expostulation. Contemplating the same bloody scene only a page earlier, Ishmael spoke, not of the angelic, but of the demonic. "If you have never seen [this] sight," he despairingly admonished us, "then suspend your decision about the propriety of devil-worship, and the expediency of conciliating the devil" (64: *250*). The contrast is too sharp to be accidental; Melville, once again, is after a meaning. The key to that meaning lies in the differing responses which Ishmael and Fleece bring to the idea of essential and intractable nature. Ishmael, at this point in *Moby-Dick,* is intellectually and emotionally incapable of accepting the fact that sharks are sharks. Evidently, nothing less than the absolute extirpation of the sharks' very nature would satisfy him. His residual Christianity makes him feel that only by ceasing to be sharks, only by disobeying themselves, could the sharks transcend the "diabolism" (64: *249*) which he sees them as representing. Since such a solution is impossible, Ishmael despairs, preparing to acknowledge the malign and bow to the demonic in life.

Fleece, in sharp contrast, imperturbably accepts essential nature. Voraciousness, in sharks and in humans, "is natur, and can't be helped." Then, in a crucial turn of thought, Fleece postulates the idea, not of self-disobedience, not of extirpation, but of *government:* "…but to gobern dat wicked natur, dat is de pint." The old man makes it clear that "government" is not the source of good, but rather only the *means* by which good is brought into being. In contrast to the radical dualism implicit in Ishmael's response to the feasting sharks, Fleece reveals himself as a monist, asserting that good and evil do *not* spring from distinct sources or from discrete vitalities, but rather from the same source and the same vitality. "You is sharks, sartin," he tells his congregation; "but if you gobern de shark in you, why den you be angel; *for all angel is not'ing more dan de shark well goberned"* (italics mine). It is, to say the least, disconcerting to conceive of the angelic choirs as consisting of rank upon rank of seraphic predators and cherubic carnivores. It is even more disconcerting to conceive of the God of Hosts as a Benign Shark, a Deific Cannibal. But this is precisely what old Fleece means. He is postulating sharkishness, the ineluctably rapacious life-dynamism of the self-sustaining individual, as the bedrock of animate creation, the raw stuff from which moral vitality—either Ahabian or Ishmaelian—must be made if it is to be made at all. He is saying that *both* good and evil spring from one source: sharkishness. He is explicitly rejecting

Father Mapple's Christian idea of extirpation—the obsessive and foredoomed effort to eliminate absolutely the vicious, the nasty, or the simply unpleasant aspects of essential nature. Fleece knows that the extirpation of sharkishness would be the extirpation of good. Just as, to Ishmael, Queequeg is "George Washington cannibalistically developed" (10: 52), so the angel is the shark morally developed. The good man is simply the good shark. This is the burden of Fleece's sermon.[3]

[3]The ontological equivalence of sharks and angels is suggested in *Mardi* where, after describing Jarl's obsessive hatred of sharks, the narrator remarks: "Yet this is all wrong. As well hate a seraph, as a shark. Both were made by the same hand." See Northwestern-Newberry *Mardi: And a Voyage Thither*, p. 40.

Herman Melville's *Moby-Dick*[1]

by Jean-Paul Sartre

...Let's not call *Moby-Dick* "this masterpiece." Let's call it instead—as we call *Ulysses*—"this imposing monument." If you enter this world, what will strike you first is its total absence of color. It's a furrowed, battered, bristly world of rugged places and reliefs, enormous fixed or moving waves. But the sea in it is neither green nor blue; it is gray, black, or white. White above all, when the boats are dancing on "the curdled milk of the whale's dreadful wrath." The sky is white, the nights are white, the icicles hang from the ship's poop "like the white tusks of a giant elephant." In Melville's work, whiteness returns like a leitmotiv of demoniacal horror. Ahab, the accursed captain, says of himself, "I leave a white and troubled wake of pallid cheeks and waters everywhere I sail." It's that "nature doesn't fail to use whiteness as an element of terror." Colors are only secondary qualities, *trompe-l'oeil.* Melville suffers from a very special kind of color blindness: he is condemned to strip things of their colored appearance, condemned to see white. Giono tells us that this sailor "has a precision of gaze which fastens onto every place where there is nothing: in the sky, in the sea, in space...." And it's true that Melville's vision is strangely precise. But it isn't nothingness he's looking at but pure being, the secret whiteness of being; he "looks upon...the universe's leprous skin, the gigantic white shroud that

An excerpt from "Herman Melville's *Moby-Dick*," by Jean-Paul Sartre. From Volume II of *The Writings of Jean-Paul Sartre,* edited by Michel Contat and Michel Rybalka and translated by Richard McCleary (Evanston: Northwestern University Press, 1974), pp. 138-40. Copyright © 1970 by Editions Gallimard; copyright © 1974 by Northwestern University Press. Reprinted by permission of the publishers.

[1]Originally published in 1941 as a review of Jean Giono's translation of *Moby-Dick.* The first paragraph and two additional sentences dealing with Giono have been omitted. The translator's version of *Moby-Dick* is at variance with Melville's language [editor's note] .

wraps all things, with a naked eye." I am reminded of that contrary yet identical expression of Audiberti's, "the secret blackness of milk." Black and white are the same here, in a Hegelian identity of opposites. The reason is that "the whole of divine nature is painted simply." At their center, on the level of their sheer existence, beings are indifferently black or white: black in their compact and stubborn isolation, white when they are struck by the light's great emptiness. It is on the level of this massive, polar indistinction of substance that the deeper drama of *Moby-Dick* is played out. Melville is condemned to live at the level of being. "All objects," he writes, "all visible objects are no more than cardboard dummies. But in each event...in living being...behind the incontestable fact, something unknown and reasoning reveals itself, behind the dummy which does not itself reason." No one more than Hegel and Melville has sensed that the absolute is there all around us, formidable and familiar, that we can see it, white and polished like a sheep bone, if we only cast aside the multicolored veils with which we've covered it. We haunt the absolute; but no one, to my knowledge, no one except Melville, has attempted this extraordinary undertaking of retaining the indefinable taste of a pure quality—the purest quality, whiteness—and seeking in that taste itself the absolute which goes beyond it. If this is one of the directions in which contemporary literature is trying in a groping way to go, then Melville is the most "modern" writer.

That is why we should stop seeing a symbolic universe in the tales he tells and in the *things* he describes. Symbols are attached retrospectively to ideas we begin with, but to begin with Melville has no idea to express. He is acquainted only with things, and it is in the depths of things that he finds his ideas. I am sure that he began by thinking that he would tell the best story of a whale hunt he could. This accounts for a first, heavily documentary aspect of his book. He tries to make even the slightest detail precise; he piles up knowledge and statistics to such a degree that he comes to seem insanely erudite and we think at first—as a result of his naively didactic concerns, the slow peaceful pace of his narrative, and also a certain humor typical of the period—that we are in the presence of some eccentric Jules Verne novel, *Twenty Thousand Leagues Across the Sea, or The Adventures of A Whale Hunter.* And then, little by little, a cancerous proliferation begins to swell and warp the clean and easy style of this American Jules Verne, just as *Crime and Punishment* is basically only a cancer eating away *Les Mysteres de Paris.* The documentary comes apart at the seams. What happened was that Melville suddenly realized that there was an idea in the whale hunt; he saw "in a white heat" that strange tie between man and animal, the *hunt.* A relationship of dizziness and death. And it is this relationship that is revealed abruptly at the end of the first hundred pages. Hatred. *Moby-Dick*'s romantic subject is the exact opposite of that of *Une Passion dans le desert:* not an animal's love for a man but a man's hatred for an animal. Ahab, the captain of the *Pequod,* has lost his leg in "the ivory jaws" of a white whale which has escaped his harpoon. Since then he has been consumed with hatred for this monster; he pursues him everywhere across the seas. This demoniacal character, whose role is to bring out what might be called the zoological side of man's fate, man's animal roots, his carnivorous nature, his nature as the scourge of animals, remains in spite of everything at the level of a somewhat outmoded romanticism: Ahab inveigles his harpooners into a solemn oath which reminds us a little of the casting of the bullets in *Der Freischütz* and of Weber's music. But this novel of hatred swells and then bursts beneath the thrust of a different cancer. With it, even the novelistic form of the narrative disappears; for there is an idea of hatred just as there is an idea of whiteness or of the whale hunt, and this idea involves the whole man, the whole human condition. From now on the novelist's technique seems to Melville to be insufficient to catch this idea. All means are going to seem legitimate to him: sermons, courtroom oratory, theatrical dialogues, interior monologues, real or seeming erudition, the epic—the epic above all. The epic because the volume of these sumptuous marine sentences, which rise up and fall away like liquid mountains dissipating into strange and superb images, is above all epic. In his best moments, Melville has the inspiration of a Lautreamont. And then, finally, he becomes conscious of writing an epic. He amuses himself writing it, he multiplies invocations to the democratic god and prosopopoeias, he entertains himself by presenting the harpooners as Homeric heroes. But when the reader has finally gotten the idea, when he finds himself at last face to face with the unaccommodated fate of man, when he sees man as Melville sees him—this fallen transcendence in his horrible abandonment—it's no longer an epic he thinks he has read but an enormous *summa,* a gigantic, monstrous, gently antediluvian book which could only be compared, in its unmeasured hugeness, to Rabelais's *Pantagruel* or James Joyce's *Ulysses.*

View Points

Richard Chase

Ahab's is the Promethean task, and as the *Pequod* searches for Moby Dick, Ahab becomes more and more the Promethean type of hero. Modern classical scholars suppose that Prometheus was a fire-god; and so Melville considers him. In *Mardi,* Taji was described as a demigod from the sun. And in the same book Melville exclaims that it is to the sun that "we Prometheuses" must go for our source of fire. By "fire" he means the creative principle: in the same passage he speaks of "the All-Plastic Power" which pervades the universe. And he warns that "only perpetual Vestal tending" will keep the fire alive in man. For fire is a double principle: it can create and it can destroy; and without perpetual tending, the act of creation becomes itself an act of destruction.

Ahab has learned this lesson well. And, like Prometheus, he is the possessor of a secret which God, whom he addresses as "my fiery father," does not know. In the tortured and difficult chapter called "The Candles," Ahab hurls his challenge at God, who has laid His "burning finger" on the *Pequod* as it sails through an electric storm. To the corposants which light up the masts like three candles and to the lightning itself, Ahab shouts:

> I know that of me which thou knowest not of thyself, oh, thou omnipotent....Through thee, thy flaming self, my scorched eyes do dimly see it. Oh, thou foundling fire, thou hermit immemorial, thou too hast thy incommunicable riddle, thy unparticipated grief. Here again with haughty agony, I read my sire. Leap! leap up, and lick the sky! I leap with thee; I burn with thee; would fain be welded with thee; defyingly I worship thee!

Like Prometheus, Ahab "reads his sire" better than his sire can read himself. Ahab's secret, as we shall see, is the knowledge that creation becomes a destruction when the Promethean *élan* is allowed to become mechanical or to degenerate into force.

As the *Pequod* sails on toward the whale, ship and crew becoming more and more like objectifications of the will of the

From *Herman Melville: A Critical Study* by Richard Chase (New York: The Macmillan Company, 1949), pp. 45-47. Copyright © 1949 by Richard Chase. Reprinted by permission of the publisher.

"monomaniac" commander, Ahab perceives the strange dualism of mechanicalness and creativity in the ship's carpenter. The carpenter has so far descended in the scale of life that he is little more than an extension of his own technique. He "was a pure manipulator..." writes Melville,

> yet this omnitooled, open-and-shut carpenter, was, after all, no mere machine of an automaton. If he did not have a common soul in him, he had a subtle something that somehow anomalously did its duty....And this it was, this same unaccountable, cunning life-principle in him; this it was, that kept him a great part of the time soliloquizing; but only like an unreasoning wheel, which also hummingly soliloquizes.

In the fire, too, Melville discerns the paradox of creativeness and mechanicalness. We recall that in the reversion scene, when Ishmael in horror suddenly finds himself facing astern, he had been gazing into the flaming tryworks just as he lost consciousness. As Ishmael regains control of himself and the ship, Melville exclaims, "believe not the artificial fire, when its redness makes all things look ghastly." Wait, he says, for "the natural sun ...the only true lamp—all others are but liars!" And later, as the crew looks forward to the third and final lowering of the boats against Moby Dick, the following interchange occurs:

Ahab. D'ye feel brave men, brave?
Stubb. As fearless fire.
Ahab. And as mechanical.

Ahab knows that his fiery father, though in fatal control of the *Pequod,* is transcended by a greater power from which the fiery father derives whatever of creativeness he has. Again we hear the suffering Prometheus who taunts Zeus: "there is some unsuffusing thing beyond thee, thou clear spirit, to whom all thy eternity is but time, all thy creativeness mechanical." This transcendent power Ahab calls the "sweet mother." She is the *personality* that lives in and despite the world machine, the human *élan* which survives in the iron mill of the universe and which asserts the possible existence of the human soul within the process of history or among the "sheer naked slidings of the elements," as D. H. Lawrence says in his essay on *Moby-Dick.* Sometimes the sweet mother comes to Ahab, though he believes that ultimately he is committed to the mechanico-apocalyptic aspect of the divine fire. "Come in thy lowest form of love," he can sometimes say, "and I will kneel and kiss thee." At these times, he is able to defy the annihilating god with the only weapon which can conquer him—the assertion of humanness. "In the midst of the personified impersonal, a personality stands here." Yet his premonition tells him that the act of defiance will finally rob him of personality, will turn out to be the act of suicide—that where the true Prometheus succeeded, Ahab, the false Prometheus, will fail.

Alan Heimert

In the *Pequod* Melville created a ship strikingly similar to the vessels which rode the oratorical seas of 1850. It sails under a red flag, and its crew—in all its "democratic dignity"—comprises a "deputation from all the isles of the earth." But the *Pequod* is clearly reminiscent of Longfellow's *Union;* it is put together of "all contrasting things" from the three sections of the United States: "oak and maple, and pine wood; iron, and pitch, and hemp." And the *Pequod* is manned (as we are reminded at each crucial moment in its career) by *thirty* isolatoes—all, Melville remarks, "federated along one keel."

The *Pequod's* mates, moreover, are "every one of them Americans; a Nantucketer, a Vineyarder, a Cape man." But of the three only one seems truly a New Englander or even a Northerner in terms either of the sectional iconography of the day or of Melville's own. Starbuck, who hails from the "prudent isle" of Nantucket and is ever-loyal to the commercial code of that island's "calculating people," is recognizably a Yankee. But good-humored Stubb seems a representative of that "essentially Western" spirit which Melville would attribute to the "convivial" frontiersman, Ethan Allen. Stubb's speech is not in the Cape Cod idiom; it is studded with references to "broad-footed farmers" and images and chickens and milldams. For Stubb, harpooning a whale is "July's immortal Fourth," on which he yearns for "old Orleans whiskey, or old Ohio, or unspeakable Monongahela"—not the rum associated with the genuine Yankee. The "Vineyarder," the

From *"Moby-Dick* and American Political Symbolism" by Alan Heimert, *American Quarterly,* 15 (1963), 501-502. Copyright © 1963 by the Trustees of the University of Pennsylvania. Reprinted by permission of the author and the University of Pennsylvania.

"very pugnacious" Flask, seems likewise closely related to that "fiery and intractable race" which Melville discovered in the south of Vivenza. Flask, who speaks of his "Martha's Vineyard plantation," reacts to whales in terms of the southern *code duello:*

> He seemed to think that the great Leviathans had personally and hereditarily affronted him; and therefore it was a sort of point of honor with him, to destroy them whenever encountered.

The harpooners, finally, who so "generously" supply "the muscles" for the "native American" mates, are representatives of the three races on which each of the American sections, it might be said, had built its prosperity in the early nineteenth century. Stubb's squire is an Indian; Starbuck's comes from the Pacific islands. And Flask, perched precariously on Daggoo's shoulders, seems, like the southern economy itself, sustained only by the strength of the "imperial negro."

H. Bruce Franklin

One mythic dragon or monster is mentioned again and again in *Moby-Dick*. This dragon is Leviathan, and Leviathan leads directly to the particular myth which does both order and define the action of *Moby-Dick*.

The Leviathan of Isaiah 27, of Job 3 and 41, of Psalm 74 and Psalm 104 was, according to various scholars, a crocodile, a whale, a serpent, and a megalosaurus. Whatever animal he was, he was what Melville's quotation from Isaiah in the "Extracts" indicates, a dragon: "In that day, the Lord with his sore, and great, and strong sword, shall punish Leviathan the piercing serpent, even Leviathan that crooked serpent; and he shall slay the dragon that is in the sea." Leviathan was, of course, particularly in later use, a name for Satan. But according to some skeptics, including Melville, Leviathan, like Jehovah, was originally an Egyptian, not a Hebrew, conception.

The eleventh Extract in *Moby-Dick* alludes to Moses as the creator of the Leviathan in Job; Moses' royal Egyptian upbringing was, as we saw in the last chapter, embarrassing to the apologists.

From *The Wake of the Gods: Melville's Mythology* by H. Bruce Franklin (Stanford, California: Stanford University Press, 1963), pp. 70-71, 73-74. Copyright © 1963 by the Board of Trustees of the Leland Stanford Junior University. Reprinted by permission of the publisher.

Behind Leviathan loomed the Egyptian god Set, or, to use the name given him by the Greek mythographers and generally used by Western mythographers until the late nineteenth century, Typhon. The struggle between Osiris and Typhon forms a basic part of the conception of Ahab's struggle with Moby Dick. The Egyptian myth explains much about Melville's myth, and Melville's myth, when compared with the Egyptian myth, explains much about Melville's mythology.[1]

The third word of *Moby-Dick* suggests the origin of its central myth. For Ishmael's namesake married an Egyptian (Genesis 21:21) and became a patriarch of Egypt. As Dorothée Finkelstein has shown, references to Egyptian history and mythology permeate Melville's work.[2] They are nowhere more pervasive than in *Moby-Dick*. The whale is "physiognomically a Sphinx"; Starbuck is "like a revivified Egyptian"; "the earliest standers of mastheads were the old Egyptians"; "'Ahab seemed a pyramid'"; in short, "whaling may well be regarded as that Egyptian mother, who bore offspring themselves pregnant from her womb." This Egyptian mother is Nut, the mother of Isis, who came pregnant from the womb, of Osiris, who impregnated Isis while he lay in the womb with her, and of Typhon, who was to be the eternal archnemesis of the god Osiris and of all men.

Osiris is a priest-king-god who sails the world in a ship which later becomes the constellation Argo. He hunts Typhon, who is usually represented by some kind of aquatic monster and who symbolizes the ocean and all in nature that is malignant to man. Once a year, Typhon dismembers Osiris. When this happens — the date is variously given as the autumnal equinox, the winter solstice, and the period in between — Osiris disappears for a certain length of time, which is also variously given. During this absence from earth, he rules the infernal regions and a ship sails the world bearing his coffin. During this time, also, his phallus is missing and the land lies infertile. In a vernal phallic ritual, Osiris is healed and the fertility of the land is restored. His dismemberment in the fall or winter symbolizes the seasonal disaster in nature. The seasonal resurrection of the sun causes, symbolizes, or is symbolized by his resurrection.

[1]One previous critic has related, rather enigmatically, the Osiris myth to *Moby-Dick*. See Charles Olson, *Call Me Ishmael* (New York, 1947), pp. 83, 116.

[2]See the section entitled "Belzoni and Ancient Egypt" in Dorothee Finkelstein, *Melville's Orienda* (New Haven, Conn., 1961).

Ahab is also a priest-king-god who sails the world in a ship which is equated with the constellation Argo. He also hunts. an aquatic monster who symbolizes the ocean and all in nature that is malignant to man. Once a year, for three successive years, he is dismembered by the aquatic monster which he hunts. The first two times, he also disappears for a length of time and then is healed with the advance of the sun. Ahab also is described as ruler of the infernal regions. Phallic rituals, fire worship, and infernal orgies are conducted on his ship, which also sails the world bearing a coffin.

Edgar A. Dryden

With its portrait of the artist as counterfeiter, *White-Jacket* apparently represents the logical conclusion of Melville's experiments with self-conscious form in the early novels, but the mode is neither fully justified nor completely mastered until *Moby-Dick*. Unlike its predecessors, *Moby-Dick* is almost completely self-contained and self-referring. Although anchored by the weight of its how-to-do-it material, it is always moving away from the objective or factual world and persistently calling attention to itself as fiction.

Ishmael's narrative strategy, as he understands, is grounded in a supreme fiction. He tells the story of his life in the form of interesting adventures, although he is aware that experience is composed of gratuitous events and disconnected sensations without significance or direction. This disturbing truth, which makes an orderly life impossible, usually remains hidden behind the many forms which man imposes on his world, since he convinces himself that they are inherent in the nature of experience itself. However, because the form of *Moby-Dick* is a self-consciously created one, the novel serves to undermine the traditional barriers which man has constructed between himself and his world. Ishmael's creative gestures are a reminder to man that whatever seems stable in experience has been put there by him-

From *Melville's Thematics of Form: The Great Art of Telling the Truth* by Edgar A. Dryden (Baltimore: The John Hopkins Press, 1968), pp. 83-85. Copyright © 1968 by The Johns Hopkins Press. Reprinted by permission of the publisher.

self. The hierarchical social structure aboard a well-ordered ship, the constructs of science and pseudo-science, pagan and Christian religious systems, even the concepts of space and time—all of the forms which man uses to assure himself that everything which happens follows certain laws—are revealed, in *Moby-Dick*, as "passing fables."

In his short introduction to the whaling extracts which preface the novel Ishmael destroys the reassuring but naïve assumption that the world can be explained and controlled by the collection of its facts and description of its objects. No matter how "authentic" the facts compiled by the "mere painstaking burrower and grubworm of a poor devil of a Sub-Sub" may seem, they cannot be taken for "gospel cetology" (xxxix).[1] As Ishmael will later demonstrate in detail, natural objects are a kind of hieroglyphic writing. Although apparently clear and self-explanatory, they really produce confusion rather than clarity. Their meaning is not to be found in the surfaces which they present to man, but seems to lie enigmatically behind them. You will not solve my mystery by staring at me, they seem to say; to read me you must possess something quite different from a knowledge of my surface.

For Ishmael, knowledge does not result from bringing man face to face with a collection of pure facts. It involves, paradoxically, a turning away from the factual world, a retreat into an imaginary reality where the only visible objects are literary ones, products of the imaginative realm they inhabit. As the Sub-Sub's "commentator," Ishmael seeks a more successful road to truth than those "long Vaticans and street stalls of the earth" through which the Sub-Sub has wandered "picking up whatever random allusions to whales he could anyways find in any book whatsoever, sacred or profane" (xxxix). Truth-telling books, for Ishmael, are not those which are guides to the actual world or are collections of facts about it. The Sub-Sub is mistaken in believing this. Rather, as verbal constructs, meaningful books are products of a mind which has turned away from the chaos and confusion of the world toward a contemplation of its own activity.

Surrounding and structuring Ishmael's encyclopedic treat-

---

[1]Citations are from the Hendricks House edition of *Moby-Dick*, ed. Luther S. Mansfield and Howard P. Vincent (New York, 1952). Lower case Roman numerals and Arabic numerals refer to the page; upper case Roman numerals refer to the chapter [editor's note].

ment of whaling is the metaphor of the whale as book, a device which always serves to remind the reader that he is encountering an imaginative reality which is the invention of an isolated consciousness. Correspondingly, the experiences of Ahab, the young Ishmael, and the rest of the *Pequod's* crew are not presented as a series of past events but, as the dramatic chapters complete with stage directions and soliloquies suggest, as part of a tragic drama composed by the mature narrator. This great play, moreover, is an obvious spatialization of a series of disconnected sensations and events. Contained within the creative consciousness of Ishmael are several versions of his past self which form an account of a self continuously developing through time. Like the image Narcissus saw in the fountain, Ishmael's inner exploration is the "key to it all." But because he seeks the "ungraspable phantom of life" (I, 3) in the mirror of art rather than in nature, choosing the role of teller rather than actor, he avoids the fatal plunge of Narcissus.

Pearl Chesler Solomon

Moby-Dick, which is Melville's allegory of man confronting an unFathered cosmos, has two endings. Ahab, who demands recognition from his God or from Nature, and who will sacrifice his world—the *Pequod*—to achieve his goal, leads the world to its destruction. Humanity is annihilated, and the indifferent sea rolls on. But there is a second ending to the novel. In the epilogue we learn that Ishmael is rescued by the *Rachel* which, in seeking her own lost children, "only found another orphan." The old order is past. Those who are still seeking their Father will die. Only Ishmael, cast out by his father, inured to loneliness and loss, is saved—and saved by another loser, by the now childless captain of the *Rachel,* whose own beloved sons have been lost. The old order is past, but perhaps a new one will come; perhaps a new relationship can take the place of the old familial one, one which will begin, perhaps, with the recognition that all men are now orphans.

From *Dickens and Melville in Their Time* by Pearl Chesler Solomon (New York: Columbia University Press, 1975), p. 4. Copyright © 1975 by Columbia University Press. Reprinted by permission of the publisher.

Glauco Cambon

Melville's Elizabethan asides look forward to Faulkner's italicized stream-of-consciousness passages in the course of which Thomas Sutpen and his harried family rise from the dead in Quentin Compson's voice. There has been James Joyce in between, of course; but in both *Moby-Dick* and *Absalom, Absalom!* memory modulates into imagination, and we share the experience of creation in progress.

For Ishmael is the artist in the act of telling us, and struggling to understand, his crucial experience. When his autobiography becomes the history of the *Pequod* and Ahab, he is liberated from his "hypos" for the second time, and in a deeper sense: he attains the liberation of imaginative objectivity. Thus his vanishing from the stage after a certain point does not constitute a breach of poetical continuity, but a dialectical movement that reproduces and expands the repeated transition from narrative to drama, from memory to visionary actuality, from conjuring subjectivity to conjured objectivity. It will help to recall that Chapter 32 ("Cetology") humorously describes the sizes of the various species of whales in terms of book-formats, an obvious literary metaphor, and that the allusions to the story as a book in the making (often attuned to self-mockery) abound significantly.[1]

If so, it should be possible to accept Ishmael as a *persona* of Melville, invisibly present *through* his narration when he ceases to be directly present *in* it; and that this persona, even as he ceases to have objective existence, has dramatic existence as actor-spectator of a half-remembered, half-conjured action. Ishmael is the self-ironizing writer seeking, and finally achieving, realization through self-effacement in the work of art; following him in the process, we see the poetry arise from its (cetological) materials,

From "Ishmael and the Problem of Formal Discontinuities in *Moby-Dick*" by Glauco Cambon, *Modern Language Notes*, 76 (1961), 523. Copyright © 1961 by The Johns Hopkins Press. Reprinted by permission of the publisher.

[1]See the end of chapter 32 ("Cetology"), the beginning of chapter 63 ("The Crotch"), the end of chapter 102 ("A Bower in the Arsacides"), and the passage in chapter 104 ("The Fossil Whale") that begins: "One often hears of writers that rise and swell with their subject, though it may seem but an ordinary one. How, then, with me, writing of this Leviathan?..."

and the discontinuities acquire the meaning of imaginative gestures within the context of a work in progress. They are indeed the structural equivalent of the copious hyperboles which animate Melville's baroque prose.

Harry B. Henderson III

Through two contrasting images of revolt Melville reminds the reader that the willing acquiescence of this crew is a striking exception to the usual rules of the sea. The first is the *Town-ho's* story, a tale of violent repression and successful overthrow of authority. This tale stands out in greater relief by its strategic placement at the very center of *Moby-Dick*.[1] Significantly, the tale is related during a gam between the men of the *Town-ho* and those of the *Pequod,* who "kept the secret among themselves so that it never transpired abaft the Pequod's mainmast."[2] The contrasting image is the constant opposition and resistance of Starbuck to what he perceives as Ahab's perversion of the commercial ends of their voyage. Though brought to the brink of the ultimate act of mutiny, the murder of his captain in his sleep, Starbuck's failure to act reflects his ambiguous role as an apostle at once of righteous resistance and of seasoned authority.[3] As Melville says in *The Confidence Man* of the divided consciousness which leads to such "a fall of valor," Starbuck may stand for "the moderate man, the invaluable understrapper of the wicked man."

The *Pequod,* unlike *White-Jacket's Neversink,* is not a microcosm of incipiently violent class conflict. The relations of Ahab and his crew rather exemplify a perverse form of democratic centralism than an outright despotism. The crew is not only "com-

From *Versions of the Past: The Historical Imagination in American Fiction* by Harry B. Henderson III (New York: Oxford University Press, Inc., 1974), pp. 135-136. Copyright © 1974 by Oxford University Press, Inc. Reprinted by permission.

[1]Melville, *Moby-Dick* (Indianapolis, New York, Kansas City; Bobbs-Merrill Company, 1964), Chapter LIV.

[2]*Ibid.,* p. 322.

[3]*Ibid.,* Chapter CXXIII.

manded" by Ahab, but is wooed and won to his purpose as he converts his formal authority into a nightmare vision of a Jacksonian democratic dictatorship. This unity of will—in which Ishmael shares, though he declares his allegiance is born of the "dread in [his] soul"[4]—is symbolized in the pact of "violence and revenge" against Moby Dick in which they join. Ahab uses a battery of inducements, including the customary forms of command and the lure of cash, as well as the pact of rebellion, to weld the crew into his effective instrument. Since all his means are bent to unnatural ends, however, the forms he manipulates become only empty vessels for his will.

William Faulkner

I think that the book which I put down with the unqualified thought "I wish I had written that" is *Moby-Dick*. The Greek-like simplicity of it: a man of forceful character driven by his sombre nature and his bleak heritage, bent on his own destruction and dragging his immediate world down with him with a despotic and utter disregard of them as individuals; the fine point to which the various natures caught [and passive as though with a foreknowledge of unalterable doom] in the fatality of his blind course are swept—a sort of Golgotha of the heart become immutable as bronze in the sonority of its plunging ruin; all against the grave and tragic rhythm of the earth in its most timeless phase: the sea. And the symbol of their doom: a White Whale. There's a death for a man, now; none of your patient pasturage for little grazing beasts you can't even see with the naked eye. There's magic in the very word. A White Whale. White is a grand word, like a crash of massed trumpets; and leviathan himself has a kind of placid blundering majesty in his name. And then put them together!!! A death for Achilles, and the divine maidens of Patmos to mourn him, to harp white-handed sorrow on their golden hair.

From *The Chicago Tribune* (July 16, 1927), p. 12. Copyright © 1927 by *The Chicago Tribune*. Reprinted by permission of *The Chicago Tribune*.

[4]*Ibid.*, Chapter XLI, p. 239.

M.O. Percival

...a contemporary of Ahab's, over in Denmark, underwent a variety and extremity of suffering almost, as he thought, unparalleled and then, with an insight almost unparalleled, he analyzed certain problems of suffering, including Ahab's. I refer, of course, to Sóren Kierkegaard, some of whose insights I shall make use of.

The problem is despair. The blow falls, in one or another of its countless ways; the suffering seems beyond all measure and desert; the sufferer feels himself singled out—elected, as it were, to be the sport and jest of some malevolent deity. The initial reaction is despair. For a person cut off in this way from the universal pattern and marked out as a sacrifice, there are, says Kierkegaard, two eventualities: he will become demonic or essentially religious.

For a healthy nature there would seem to be release just short of an experience essentially religious. Infinite resignation, as Kierkegaard calls it, even without Christian faith, will bring peace. In the Stoic resignation there was peace, but a hard peace, dictated by pride. There is the example of Diogenes, of whom Epictetus says: "Hadst thou seized upon his possessions, he would rather have let them go than have followed thee for them—aye, had it been even a limb." But Ahab was too passionate and self-willed to make the gesture of infinite resignation. From a child he had been rebellious. The Stoic could submit himself to Providence. He could knit his mutilated spirit into the spirit of the universe. But not Ahab. "Who's over me?" he demands of Starbuck, in response to an expostulation. Stubb, who knew him well, reports that he never saw him kneel.

There remains the Christian way of resignation, the only way, according to Kierkegaard, whereby a morbid nature, passionate and self-willed, can encounter despair and conquer it. If the sufferer can say: "Before thee, O God, I am nothing, do with me as thou wilt," he will be able to bear the burden. He can lose the self, and then, by the well-known Christian paradox, regain it.

From *A Reading of Moby-Dick* by M. O. Percival (Chicago: The University of Chicago Press, 1950), pp. 16-18. Copyright © 1950 by the University of Chicago. Reprinted by permission of the publisher.

But of Christian feeling there is no trace in Ahab. All the ways
of resignation are therefore closed.

The alternative, in Kierkegaard's analysis, is defiance. Since
the sufferer cannot lose himself, his one recourse is to affirm
himself. The despair is not thereby cured. There is despair in
the very effort to combat despair. As the consciousness of self
increases, the despair increases, while the increasing despair
increases the consciousness of self. The cycle thus set in motion
has an inevitable outcome: the sufferer becomes demonic.

An important stage in Ahab's progress from the blind rage of
complete despair to a rage partially subdued and organized under
mad direction is reached in an incident which occurred before
the *Pequod* sailed, although it is not described until long afterward. It is postponed, I suppose, in order that the element of allegory might readily be perceived. Ahab had returned home, the
Pequod was getting ready, when one night he fell and was discovered lying upon the ground, helpless and insensible. "His
ivory limb [had] been so violently displaced, that it had stake-
wise smitten, and all but pierced his groin; nor was it without
extreme difficulty that the agonizing wound was entirely cured."
In this incident we find that Moby Dick—present in the ivory
stake—had bitten into the very center of his being, leaving a
wound that was to prove incurable. But Kierkegaard would see
something more—a push toward the demonic. The incident
included a twofold psychic trauma—the initial humiliation in
his own eyes and the subsequent humiliation arising from compassion on the part of others. To be lifted out of the universal
pattern, to be an object of humiliation to one's self and an object
of compassion to others—this torture, more than any other, says
Kierkegaard, tempts man to rebel against God. It can be borne
only by resignation. But if it is combined with a passionate self-
will, "then it will end with the sufferer losing his reason." As an
instance of self-will turning the sufferer demonic, Kierkegaard
cites Richard III. Of despair referred to God and turning into
triumph, he is his own example. In the case of Ahab, it was this
fall, hushed up by the few friends who knew about it, that sent
him into a lama-like seclusion in his cabin—a seclusion from
which he did not emerge until, turned demonic, he took his place
upon the quarter-deck, prepared and determined to league his
crew into a solemn oath to seek revenge upon Moby Dick.

Michael T. Gilmore

Numerous critics have pointed out that the *Pequod* bears a striking resemblance to the American ship of state which plied the oratorical seas in Melville's day.[1] As captain of the *Pequod*, Ahab is entrusted with the fate of the national Israel, and he is himself representative of the chosen people, having wandered for "forty years on the pitiless sea."[2] Potentially, of course, he is also a type of the Savior, since it is from the seed of Israel that the Messiah is born. Melville's contemporaries believed in the messianic role of the American people, and they were persuaded, as he put it in *Mardi,* that history had entered "the last scene of the last act of her drama."[3] As recently as *Redburn,* Melville himself had said of his countrymen that "We are the heirs of all time, and with all nations we divide our inheritance. On this Western Hemisphere all tribes and people are forming into one federated whole; and there is a future which shall see the estranged children of Adam restored as to the old hearth-stone in Eden" (IV, 169). It is hardly surprising, in view of these sentiments, that in *Moby-Dick* Ishmael characterizes the polyglot crew of the *Pequod* as "an Anacharsis Clootz deputation" drawn from all the ends of the earth and "federated along one keel" under the command of an American skipper (p. 108).

It is revealing to recall in this connection the traditional iconography of Christ as a dragon slayer.[4] The Bible speaks of the sea-serpent or Leviathan that will be destroyed on the day of judgment and whose death will deliver the children of Adam

From "Melville's Apocalypse: American Millennialism and *Moby-Dick"* by Michael T. Gilmore, *ESQ: A Journal of the American Renaissance,* 21 (1975), 155-56. Copyright © 1975 by Michael T. Gilmore. Reprinted by permission of the editors.

[1]See in particular Alan Heimert, *"Moby-Dick* and American Political Symbolism," *American Quarterly,* 15 (1963), 498-534.

[2]Harrison Hayford and Hershel Parker, eds., *Moby-Dick* (New York: Norton, 1967), p. 443. All quotations are from this edition; page references are cited in the text.

[3]*The Writings of Herman Melville* (Evanston and Chicago: Northwestern University Press and the Newberry Library, 1970), III, 525. Further references to this edition will be cited by volume and page number in the text.

[4]Here I am indebted to the discussion of *Paradise Regained* in Northrop Frye, *The Return of Eden: Five Essays on Milton's Epics* (Toronto: University of Toronto Press, 1965), pp. 118-43.

from bondage to sin. An illustration is the verse from Isaiah 27 which Melville quotes in the "Extracts": "In that day, the Lord with his sore, and great, and strong sword, shall punish Leviathan the piercing serpent, even Leviathan that crooked serpent; and he shall slay the dragon that is in the sea" (p. 2). The victory over Satan, which restores mankind to Paradise, fulfills God's prophecy in Genesis that the seed of Adam shall bruise the serpent's head. It is a prophecy of special significance for the redeemer nation, and it is cited repeatedly in writings of the emigrant Puritans. Two hundred years before the sailing of the *Pequod,* for example, John Winthrop recorded in his journal that during the synod at Cambridge a snake appeared in the midst of a sermon and was promptly killed by one of the elders. Winthrop interpreted the incident as follows: "The serpent is the devil; the synod, the representative of the churches of Christ in New England. The devil had formerly and lately attempted their disturbance and dissolution; but their faith in the seed of the woman overcame him and crushed his head."[5] The step from Winthrop's confident assertion to Melville's novel is long historically but short in imaginative terms; they draw on a common conception of American destiny. Ahab begins his hunt on December 25th, the date of the Savior's birth, and he is said to have "piled upon the whale's white hump the sum of all the general rage and hate felt by his whole race from Adam down" (p. 160). The God of Genesis declares to the serpent that "thou shalt bruise his heel," and in fulfillment of the prophecy that he would be dismembered, Ahab lost his leg to Moby Dick. "I now prophesy," he vows, "that I will dismember my dismemberer" (p. 147). As he prepares to embark on his millennial quest, the hymn "There is a land of pure delight" rings "full of hope and fruition" through the cold New England air:

> Sweet fields beyond the swelling flood,
> Stand dressed in living green.
> So to the Jews old Canaan stood,
> While Jordan rolled between.   (p. 95)

The Canaan of the hymn corresponds to the Promised Land that Christ will conquer for the spiritual Israel by crushing the head of Leviathan.

[5]James Kendall Hosmer, ed., *Winthrop's Journal: "History of New England"* (New York: Barnes & Noble, 1966), II, 347-48.

Martin Leonard Pops

I think, then, that of the ways in which Moby Dick may be regarded as symbol, two of the most appropriate are as the metaphysical duality of the Cosmos and as the life-energy, sacred and sexual, of the Center. Undoubtedly the two visceral demands of Ahab's being are metaphysical and sexual: to slay God if He exists or prove His absence if He does not; and to unite with the Mother and slay as well as embrace the Father. It is Melville's great triumph that as he made the symbolic elements of the Whale literally coextensive with one another—the realm of God and Sexual Energy one—so he made Ahab's quests seamlessly coincide and both depend on the hurling of one harpoon in an ultimately definitive act. But because the value of the Romantic Quest lies not in attainment but in the struggle therefor, Ishmael, not Ahab, is the book's only successful quester. For Ishmael engages a metaphysical problem he knows he cannot solve and discovers his deepest satisfactions in a sexual relationship he cannot consummate and in a perception of the Sacred he cannot maintain. Indeed, it may even be argued, as D. H. Lawrence first argued on behalf of another American hero, Natty Bumppo,[1] that Ishmael not only does not grow older (i.e., overripe with fulfillment) as the quest continues but that he grows younger and younger. His first sexual encounter in *Moby-Dick* is adult (sleeping with Queequeg); his second is adolescent (holding hands and squeezing sperm); but his third and last is natal. For in the book's final tableau, Ishmael emerges from the creamy pool as if reborn, and, like Nature herself ("The unharming sharks...with padlocks on their mouths"), he too experiences, in the cataclysm of death and rebirth, the real, if transient, peace of exhaustion. For Ishmael avoids the fate of the manic quester: crashing against or through the walls of dissatisfaction, a route that leads, inevitably, to further and further dissatisfaction. The very uncertainties of existence keep Ishmael young, and in the tensions of unfulfillment, he achieves a measure of real happiness.

From *The Melville Archetype* by Martin Leonard Pops (Kent, Ohio: The Kent State University Press, 1970), p. 87. Copyright © 1970 by Martin Leonard Pops. Reprinted by permission of the publisher.

[1]D. H. Lawrence, *Studies in Classic American Literature* (New York, 1923), pp. 62-64.

Lawrance Thompson

He [Melville] was temperamentally and artistically inclined to strike the Byronic pose and rebaptize himself, not in the name of the Father, but in the name of Satan. Even if we are forced to see in Melville's sophomoric attitude a certain indication of arrested development, it is better to recognize him for what he was than to inflate his attitude into something which it was not.

Baldly stated, then, Melville's underlying theme in *Moby-Dick* correlates the notions that the world was put together wrong and that God is to blame; that God in his infinite malice asserts a sovereign tyranny over man and that most men are seduced into the mistaken view that this divine tyranny is benevolent and therefore acceptable; but that the freethinking and enlightened and heroic man will assert the rights of man and will rebel against God's tyranny by defying God in thought, word, deed, even in the face of God's ultimate indignity, death.

Chronology of Important Dates

	Melville	*The Age*
1819	1 August born in New York City to Allan and Maria Gansevoort Melville.	The nation suffers its first real economic depression.
1820		Passage of the Missouri Compromise.
1828		Election of Andrew Jackson.
1832	Allan Melville dies following bankruptcy and mental collapse. The Melville family had moved to Albany two years earlier. Melville clerks and teaches in the vicinity for seven years.	
1836		Publication of Emerson's *Nature*.
1837		The Panic of 1837 causes numerous financial failures and widespread economic distress.
1839	Sails for Liverpool on the merchant ship *St. Lawrence*.	
1841	Ships from Fairhaven (New Bedford) on the whaler *Acushnet* for the South Seas.	
1844	Returns home aboard the frigate *United States*.	
1846	*Typee* published.	War with Mexico.

Melville	*The Age*
1847	*Omoo.* Marries Elizabeth Shaw, daughter of Chief Justice Lemuel Shaw of Massachusetts, and settles in New York City.	
1849	*Mardi* and *Redburn.* Travels in Europe.	
1850	*White-Jacket.* Moves to Pittsfield, Massachusetts, where he begins writing of "a whaling voyage." Forms friendship with Hawthorne, to whom he subsequently dedicates *Moby-Dick* "in token of my admiration for his genius."	Hawthorne's *The Scarlet Letter.* Passage of the Fugitive Slave Law as a provision of the Compromise of 1850.
1851	18 October *Moby-Dick* published in England as *The Whale,* then in the United States under its present title.	
1852	*Pierre.*	
1854		Thoreau's *Walden.* The Kansas-Nebraska Act repeals the Missouri Compromise and sanctions the spread of slavery north of the line 36° 30'.
1855	*Israel Potter.*	Whitman publishes *Leaves of Grass.*
1856	*The Piazza Tales.* Travels in Europe and the Holy Land.	
1857	*The Confidence-Man.* Returns to the United States.	
1861		Outbreak of the Civil War.
1863	Moves back to New York City.	
1865		Lee surrenders to Grant at Appomattox. Lincoln assassinated.

	Melville	*The Age*

1866   *Battle-Pieces and Aspects of the War.* Appointed Inspector of Customs at the Port of New York, a post he held until his resignation on the last day of 1885.

1869   Twain's *The Innocents Abroad.* Formation of the Knights of Labor.

1876   *Clarel* published at the expense of his uncle Peter Gansevoort.

1886   The Haymarket Riot.

1888   *John Marr and Other Sailors* privately printed.

1890   Closing of the frontier.

1891   *Timoleon* privately printed. 28 September Melville dies in New York City.

1924   *Billy Budd* first published.

Notes on the Editor and Contributors

MICHAEL T. GILMORE, the editor, is Assistant Professor of English at Brandeis University.

NEWTON ARVIN, the author of books on Hawthorne, Whitman, and Melville, was Professor of English at Smith College.

W. H. AUDEN, the Anglo-American poet, died in 1973. His *Thank You, Fog: Last Poems* was published in 1974.

GLAUCO CAMBON is the author of several critical studies, including *Dante's Craft* (1969) and *Eugenio Montale* (1972). He edited the volume on Pirandello in the *Twentieth Century Views* series.

RICHARD CHASE was Professor of English at Columbia University. He published numerous articles and books on American literature, including an influential study of *The American Novel and Its Tradition* (1957).

EDGAR A. DRYDEN, the author of *Melville's Thematics of Form* (1968), is Associate Professor of English at the State University of New York, Buffalo.

WILLIAM FAULKNER was awarded the Nobel Prize for Literature in 1950.

H. BRUCE FRANKLIN teaches English at Rutgers University. His most recent book is *Back Where You Came From* (1975).

ALAN HEIMERT, author of *Religion and the American Mind* (1966), is Powell M. Cabot Professor of American Literature at Harvard University.

HARRY B. HENDERSON III, author of *Versions of the Past* (1974), was Assistant Professor of Literature at the State University of New York.

DANIEL HOFFMAN, poet and critic, teaches English at the University of Pennsylvania. His books include *The Poetry of Stephen Crane* (1957), *Form and Fable in American Fiction* (1961), and *Poe, Poe, Poe, Poe, Poe, Poe, Poe* (1972).

LEWIS MUMFORD, distinguished critic and essayist, is the author of some twenty books.

CHARLES OLSON, philosopher and poet, died in 1970. While a graduate student at Harvard in 1934, he located Melville's collection of Hawthorne's works and his seven-volume edition of Shakespeare. Melville's annotations and underlinings in Shakespeare's plays supplied the inspiration for *Call Me Ishmael* (1947).

M. O. PERCIVAL, author of *A Reading of Moby-Dick* (1950), taught at the University of Chicago.

MARTIN LEONARD POPS is the author of *The Melville Archetype* (1970).

JEAN-PAUL SARTRE, the eminent philosopher, playwright, and novelist, declined the Nobel Prize for Literature in 1964.

RICHARD SLOTKIN, author of *Regeneration Through Violence* (1973), teaches English at Wesleyan University.

HENRY NASH SMITH was Professor of English at the University of California, Berkeley, until his recent retirement. He is the author of *Virgin Land* (1950) and *Mark Twain* (1962).

PEARL CHESLER SOLOMON, author of *Dickens and Melville in Their Times* (1975), teaches English at The City College of The City University of New York.

LAWRANCE THOMPSON was Professor of English at Princeton University. He wrote books on Faulkner, Frost, Longfellow, and Melville.

ROBERT ZOELLNER, author of *The Salt-Sea Mastodon* (1973), is Professor of English at Colorado State University.

Selected Bibliography

Ausband, Stephen C., "The Whale and the Machine: An Approach to *Moby-Dick*," *American Literature,* 47 (May 1975), 197-211.

Baird, James, *Ishmael.* Baltimore: Johns Hopkins University Press, 1956.

Brodtkorb, Paul Jr., *Ishmael's White World: A Phenomenological Reading of Moby-Dick.* New Haven: Yale University Press, 1965.

Foster, Charles H., "Something in Emblems: A Reinterpretation of *Moby-Dick," New England Quarterly,* 34 (March 1961), 3-35.

Hillway, Tyrus, and Luther S. Mansfield, eds., *Moby-Dick Centennial Essays.* Dallas: Southern Methodist University Press, 1953.

Horsford, Howard C., "The Design of the Argument in *Moby-Dick," Modern Fiction Studies,* 8 (Autumn 1962), 233-51.

Parker, Hershel, and Harrison Hayford, eds., *Moby-Dick as Doubloon: Essays and Extracts (1851-1970).* New York: Norton, 1970.

Paul, Sherman, "Melville's 'The *Town Ho's* Story,'" *American Literature,* 21 (May 1949), 212-21.

Pavese, Cesare, "The Literary Whaler," trans. B. M. Arnett, *Sewanee Review,* 68 (Summer 1960), 407-18.

Ross, Morton, *"Moby-Dick* as an Education," *Studies in the Novel,* 6 (Spring 1974), 62-75.

Shulman, Robert, "The Serious Functions of Melville's Phallic Jokes," *American Literature,* 33 (May 1961), 179-94.

Stewart, George R., "The Two *Moby-Dicks," American Literature,* 25 (January 1954), 417-48.

Vincent, Howard P., *The Trying-Out of Moby-Dick.* Boston: Houghton Mifflin, 1949; reprinted Carbondale: Southern Illinois University Press, 1965.

Watters, R. E., "The Meanings of the White Whale," *University of Toronto Quarterly*, 20 (January 1951), 155-68.

Woodson, Thomas, "Ahab's Greatness: Prometheus as Narcissus," *ELH, A Journal of English Literary History*, 33 (September 1966), 351-69.

The following studies contain analyses of *Moby-Dick:*

Berthoff, Warner, *The Example of Melville.* Princeton: Princeton University Press, 1962.

Bowen, Merlin, *The Long Encounter: Self and Experience in the Writings of Herman Melville.* Chicago: University of Chicago Press, 1960.

Brumm, Ursula, *American Thought and Religious Typology*, trans. John Hoaglund. New Brunswick: Rutgers University Press, 1970.

Chase, Richard, *The American Novel and Its Tradition.* Garden City: Doubleday, 1957.

Donoghue, Denis, *Thieves of Fire.* London: Faber & Faber, 1973.

Feidelson, Charles Jr., *Symbolism and American Literature.* Chicago: University of Chicago Press, 1953.

Fiedler, Leslie A., *Love and Death in the American Novel*, rev. ed. New York: Dell, 1966.

Fussell, Edwin, *Frontier: American Literature and the American West.* Princeton: Princeton University Press, 1965.

Kaul, A. N., *The American Vision: Actual and Ideal Society in Nineteenth-Century Fiction.* New Haven: Yale University Press, 1963.

Lebowitz, Alan, *Progress into Silence: A Study of Melville's Heroes.* Bloomington: Indiana University Press, 1970.

Levin, Harry, *The Power of Blackness: Poe, Hawthorne, Melville.* New York: Knopf, 1958.

Lewis R. W. B., *The American Adam: Innocence, Tragedy, and Tradition in the Nineteenth Century.* Chicago: University of Chicago Press, 1955.

Marx, Leo, *The Machine in the Garden: Technology and the Pastoral Ideal in America.* New York: Oxford University Press, 1964.

Matthiessen, F. O., *American Renaissance: Art and Expression in the Age of Emerson and Whitman.* New York: Oxford University Press, 1941.

Rosenberry, Edward, *Melville and the Comic Spirit.* Cambridge, Mass.: Harvard University Press, 1955.

Sedgwick, William E., *Herman Melville: The Tragedy of Mind.* Cambridge, Mass.: Harvard University Press, 1944.

Seelye, John, *Melville: The Ironic Diagram.* Evanston: Northwestern University Press, 1970.

Wadlington, Warwick, *The Confidence Game in American Literature.* Princeton: Princeton University Press, 1975.